Understanding Today's

Youth

Daniel O. Aleshire

Convention Press / Nashville, Tennessee

Church Training Department
Sunday School Board, SBC
127 Ninth Avenue North
Nashville, Tennessee 37234

Contents

Photograph Credits: Clyde Denton Jr. 12, 15, and 49; Nancy Robinson 24, and 32; Jim Sweeney 41, 44, 57, 63, 71, 81, 103, 104, and 124-125; Paul Buddle 89; Regina Ranish 98 and 99, 120; Gunter Wall 136.

cAbout the Author

Daniel O. Aleshire has had a variety of experiences in Baptist life. He has served Baptist churches as pastor, interim pastor, associate pastor, minister of youth, and interim minister of administration and education. Also, Dan has served as director of the Baptist Student Union at George Peabody College in Nashville.

From 1975 through 1978, he was employed as a research scientist at Search Institute, Minneapolis, Minnesota. Presently, he is associate professor of psychology and christian education at Southern Baptist Theological Seminary, Louisville, Kentucky.

His impressive credentials might make a person think Dan is a "stuffed shirt." He does have a wealth of knowledge, but with it he blends warmth, understanding, and strength of character.

Foreword

This book has been written with the hope that it will benefit people who care about youth and work with them in churches. I have tried carefully to document the sources of the ideas as they appear, but wish to cite three contributors because of their significant influence on the project.

The first is the forty youth with whom I spent several Sunday evenings, and who are valuable members of my church. Each chapter begins with an edited transcript of our discussions. Their concerns became the basis for determining which of many possible topics would be included in the chapters that follow.

A second source consists of a group of texts on adolescent psychology: by John Conger; B. F. Rothschild, R. Altland, and L. B. Green; and Dorothy Rogers. They are excellent sources of current thought and research in adolescent psychology.

A third source is the work of Merton Strommen, with whom I had the pleasure of working for several years, and whose ideas about youth and youth ministry no doubt appear in these chapters more frequently than the footnotes would indicate.

Two important studies of youth are extensively used in this book. The first is an ongoing study called *Monitoring the Future*. It is a project of the Institute of Social Research of the University of Michigan, with primary funding provided by the National Institute on Drug Abuse.

The second study includes only Southern Baptist youth and reports their response on two youth ministry surveys: the *Youth Research Survey* and *Becoming the Gift*. Both tools were developed by Search Institute, Minneapolis, Minnesota, with Merton Strommen as principal designer. The data for Southern Baptists from 1970-81, which are reported in this text, were made available from the archival files of Search Institute.

Thanks are due to my family who accepted my excessive absences during the production of this volume, to the competent staff of the Youth Section of the Church Training Department who have helped along the way, to my colleagues H. Steven Shoemaker and Paul Schmidt who read drafts and provided helpful comments; and to Mrs. Peggy Shaw who typed and retyped the manuscript.

Daniel Aleshire
Louisville, Kentucky

Introduction:
Growing Up

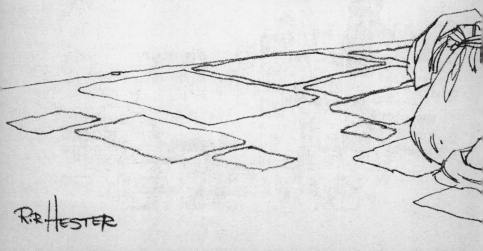

R.R. Hester

1

Introduction: Growing Up

The New Testament mentions only one incident from the life of Jesus as an adolescent. In that passage, he was in trouble with his parents. Jesus had remained in the Jerusalem Temple without telling his parents what he was going to do. His mother confronted him after a three-day search: "Son, why have you treated us so? . . . Your father and I have been looking for you anxiously" (Luke 2:48, RSV).[1] Doesn't that sound like a mother? What youth has escaped teenage years and not been similarly confronted by an exasperated parent? "We've been worried about you. Couldn't you have called to tell us that you were going to stay? How could you do this to us?"

Jesus' response was no less familiar. "Did you not know that I must be in my Father's house?" (Luke 2:49, RSV) he said, his voice cracking on its way to manhood. What parent has reared an adolescent and never heard his child utter a similar lament: "You don't understand me. You just don't understand."

The Scripture continues. "And they *(his parents)* did not understand the saying which he spoke to them" (Luke 2:50, RSV). Jesus' parents weren't alone. Most parents have a hard time understanding adolescents. Of course, young Jesus was making a theological statement in this passage, and it flew right past his parents' ability to understand. Most adolescents, however, have a way of making statements about thoughts and feelings that completely elude parental understanding. "You just aren't making any sense," plead parents in frustration.

The familiarity of the passage abruptly ended when Jesus "went down with them . . . to Nazareth, and was obedient to them" (2:51, RSV). Who ever heard of such a thing? An adolescent who day in and day out was obedient. Jesus really was one-of-a-kind ("only begotten"—John 3:16) wasn't he? Imagine the drama: the Word became flesh and lived among us; and even as his legs grew, his voice cracked, his beard sprouted, and his muscles thickened, he obeyed his parents.

Jesus was an adolescent, a misunderstood disturber of parental plans, a youth who obeyed parents and beyond them, obeyed the Father.

Other precocious youth emerge from the Scriptures.

Young David was taking care of the family flock while his older brothers had gone off to battle the Philistines. David wandered into the Israeli camp about the time the whole battle had ground to a halt. The enemy had produced a weapon that Israeli intelligence didn't know how to handle—a giant named Goliath. David's older brother, Eliab, heard David asking about the stalemate. "Eliab's anger was kindled against David, and he said, 'why have you come down? And with whom have you left those few sheep in the wilderness?'" (1 Sam. 17:28, RSV). Isn't that just like two brothers? The older one assumed the younger one didn't know what he was doing. Even though the battle with the enemy was at a standstill, two brothers easily got a family battle going.

David's response to his older brother was classic: "What have I done now?" (v. 29) How many parents have gone to the scene of two brothers in an argument only to hear one or the other say, "I wasn't doing anything!" As in ancient Israel, families in modern America are environments where brotherly wills clash, where cross words fire, and no one is altogether sure why.

Then David did what young men frequently have done. He said, "Let no man's heart fail because of him; your servant will go and fight with this Philistine" (v. 32). What a rash, bold, and unbelievable remark! Youth seem to have an exuberance that doesn't know when to stop. Something wants to push for the limit. The giants, just like

Goliath, are funny looking and awesome. For American youth, the giant to conquer may be a 100-mile-per-hour-gallop on the interstate, or balancing precariously at the edge of a cliff on the wrong side of the protective railing.

Of course, David's boast was not merely a macho threat. It was the act of faith of a person who did not have the maturity to calculate the odds of success. (David did grow up and learn to calculate odds, and Uriah paid a price for it. Maturity is not always an improvement on youth.)

David confronted Goliath with these words: "I come to you in the name of the Lord of hosts, . . . This day the Lord will deliver you into my hand, . . . that all the earth may know that there is a God in Israel, and that all this assembly may know that the Lord saves not with sword and spear; for the battle is the Lord's and he will give you into our hand" (1 Sam. 17:45-47, RSV).

Maybe it was youthful curiosity that nudged David off the hillside down to the battle camp. Maybe it was sibling rivalry that had Eliab ready to pounce on his young brother. But, there with a pimple on his face and the beginning of hair on his chest, David found the way of faith, swung the sling, hurled the rock, and killed the giant.

Faith does blossom in the midst of adolescent life. Youth are capable of faith, of gallantry, of service, of sacrifice. But there are a lot of Eliab's around who keep telling them to go back to the hillside, keep their sheep and their silence, and stay out of the way.

Twenty-eight generations later, David's youthful descendent Joseph found himself engaged to a very pregnant teenage Mary. Joseph wondered what was the honorable thing to do (Matt. 1:19-21). A little educated, little privileged, little understood Mary, responded to the pregnancy with poetry:

> My soul magnifies the Lord,
> And my spirit rejoices in God my Savior,
> For he has regarded the low estate of his
>   handmaiden . . .
> For he who is mighty has done great things
>   for me,
> And holy is his name.
>
> (Luke 1:46-49, RSV)

Mary found words as the babe grew within her. Words always came hard for her—as they do for many adolescent girls. At Jesus' birth, "Mary kept all these things, pondering them in her heart" (Luke 2:19, RSV). Maturity came fast and hard as her true-gift-to-the-world Son reached adulthood. But maturity could never bring the poetry her adolescence did. She continued to ponder the Miracle that grew up in her home. The delicacy of her pondering was never more dear than when as a birth-exhausted girlish mother, she absorbed the gifts of life, the Messiah, angel choirs, and strange shepherds who came in the night.

The Bible has surprisingly little to say about the period of life Americans call "adolescence." It does, however, say a great deal through the lives of teenaged believers who sought the Father, troubled parents, fought with brothers, lived with faith, wondered about the right, and responded to life with poetry and ponderings.

This book is about youth. It is intended for persons who are working with youth in the real world of local congregations. There in Sunday School, Church Training, Youth choir, Pioneers, and Acteens youth hear of God's grace and call to service. There, they have opportunity to give themselves in the name of the Christ.

This book is about the youth who cut up in Sunday School, forget to prepare their assignment in Church Training, tease the fair-haired soprano in choir, and talk about boys instead of missionaries during Acteens' meetings. It seeks to be a book about real youth struggling with the realities of American life.

This book draws upon three resources for understanding youth and youth ministry.

The first is the broad themes of Scripture. While there are a few passages that say, "Treat youth in this way or that," there are only a few. This book cannot claim a focus text for every point. There are no major points of advice or concern which do not grow from the overwhelming stances of Scripture. For example, leaders of youth are encouraged to love the youth with whom they work. There is no text, Old Testament or New, that commands leaders to love youth. There is, however, the inescapable affirmation that Christians are called to "love one another" (1 John 4:7). Following the general command to all Christians will help some Christians be effective youth leaders.

Part of this book suggests ways in which love is best expressed to youth. These parts cannot cite a passage that says: "Love youth by being real, available, open to them, and patient with them." Scripture does provide a list of qualities that should characterize the maturing believer, and some of these include: patience, kindness,

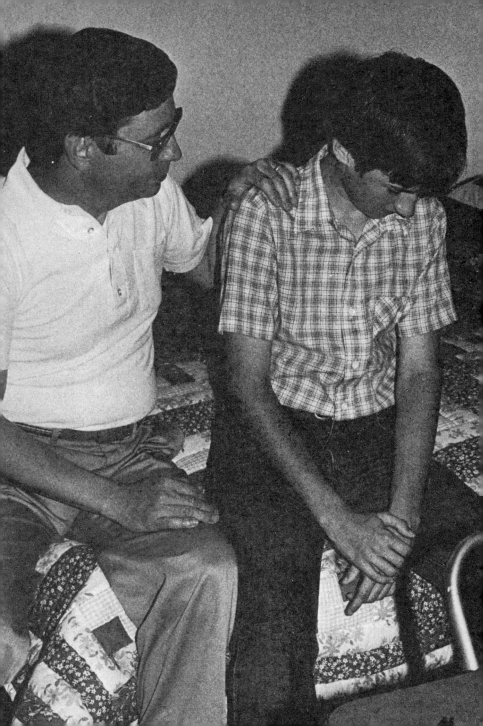

goodness, faithfulness, gentleness (Gal. 5:22-23). The way leaders of youth love youth most effectively is by exhibiting the fruit of the Spirit in their lives. Maturing in the qualities of grace, given by the Spirit, will make leaders of youth effective—but that kind of maturing will make any Christian a more able believer.

A second resource is psychological and sociological literature. Some fundamental understandings of what youth are like, the problems they face, the hurts they uniquely experience, and the events which affect their lives are best revealed by psychological and sociological research. This kind of information is most helpful at the point of diagnosis and understanding. It is least authoritative, for Christian believers, at the point of prescribing what should be done. The ultimate prescriptions of life emerge from God's revelation.

A third resource is my own experience and acquaintance with youth. Each chapter begins with an excerpt from discussions which formed the basis of this volume. Most of the issues explored in it grew out of what the youth expressed in those meetings. Youth are an important resource in a project such as this. Just as Scripture is its own best interpreter, youth frequently are their own best interpreters. I take youth seriously. Ministry is not something that can be done for them; it is something done with them.

This book has one image that winds its way through the chapters: "growing up." Those are words many of you may have spoken when you saw a friend or relative for the first time in four years. The last time you saw that person, his/her nine-year-old girl and ten-year-old boy were merrily chasing through childhood. This time you saw a thirteen-year-old girl whose womanhood was beginning to flourish, and a fourteen-year-old boy who seemed a foot taller. You looked at them and said, "You have really grown up." They were embarrassed.

"Growing up" is a phrase that describes the whole process of moving from infancy to adulthood. Frequently it takes on a distinct meaning when child-like characteristics give way to adult-like appearance. Youth are *growing up;* they are making a turn that takes them down an irreversible road to adulthood. *Growing up* includes the time when children begin to do things independently, when they go off with their friends and experiment with adult games and pains. *Growing up* involves the dramatic years of life when almost everything changes, at least a little. *Growing up* requires understanding, patience, and the willingness to be both gentle and firm. This is a book about youth who are growing up.

Personal Learning Activities

How are youth today like David? *They have the same youthful curiosity and may ask when challenged what have I done now.*

How are we as adults somewhat like Eliab in our relationships with youth? *We assume to often they don't know what their doing. We get angry & impatient.*

The author lists the resources out of which he has written this book. What resources/experiences in relationship to youth do you bring to this study? *I have taught Bible study for 5 yrs. to a youth group. I've taught Sunday School jr & sr. high for over 12 yrs. Was Bible*

Someone has said, "You can give without loving, but you cannot love without giving." The symbol used throughout this book represents *agape,* or Christian love (sacrificial, self-giving care). Re-read the author's comments about biblical guidelines for adults in relating to youth.

resource person for girl guards to earn their badges girls 12-18. Was chairmen for our mission group in Pd. for 5 yrs where I did mission study & Bible study.

Growing Up American

2

Growing Up American

LEADER:	Let's get acquainted. Tell me one fact about you that you would like me to know.
DAVID:	I'm David, and I'm a wrestler.
YOUTH:	Yeah, he tried to tackle me once. *(Some nervous laughter followed this remark.)*
CATHY:	My name is Cathy.
YOUTH:	She's a Leonardo.
LEADER:	What's a Leonardo?
YOUTH:	It's a girl! *(Several youth loudly agree.)*
BECKY:	My name is Becky. I don't know any facts about me.
YOUTH:	She's the mascot at Kammarer School.
LEADER:	What's a mascot do?
BECKY:	I dress up in a costume and run around and get the crowd excited at the basketball games.
LEADER:	Next.
JENNIFER:	I'm Jennifer, and I play basketball for the girl's team.

CHUCK:	My name is Chuck. I'm related to Leonardo. She's weird, she's made of all natural materials.
LEADER:	I asked for facts. *(laughter)* I guess a fact about you, Chuck, is that you tell stories about your sister!
YOUTH:	No, he's originally from another planet *(giggles)*.
LEADER:	Really? Who's next?
SARAH:	My name is Sarah, and I'm a cheerleader.
LEADER:	That's two cheerleaders!
YOUTH:	We have two basketball players, two cheerleaders, a gymnast, and somebody from another planet.
LEADER:	A lot of jocks in this room, huh?
YOUTH:	Yeah, and an alien, a wrestler, and one nice person. *(giggles, laughter)*

_____

The script is from a drama performed in a twelve-by-twelve Baptist church meeting room at six o'clock on Sunday evening. I met with the middle school youth for the first time, and asked them to tell me their names and a fact about themselves. As they answered the question, the drama unfolded. Before we were five minutes into the evening, there had been a few periods of nervous, puzzled silence; innumerable giggles, wiggles, and knowing glances between friends; and a sense of fear-joy-excitement bundled into one package as only youth can assemble them.

They were good youth—growing up in America, Sunday-night-at-church youth. They were people for whom Christ died and who, when they weren't wiggling or squirming, knew that.

In the succeeding four weeks, they told of dreams, fears, horrors, and hardships. They always told their story above the noise of chatter. They always found our subject more difficult to focus on than any other thought that came flying through the room.

We almost lost the conversation altogether the night a bug showed up in the room. The girls screamed although they weren't afraid; and the boys battled off the intruder like knights facing a dragon in a medieval bout.

They were youth: too noisy, too easily distracted, trying to fit into bodies that were changing too quickly, or not quickly enough. They were middle-school youth: experimenting with adult-like feelings and retreating to childlike behavior.

They were Baptist youth Grady Nutt was the only preacher who never bored them; they preferred the balcony to the main floor; they wondered what baptism meant. And between the wiggles and giggles, they were creative, insightful, scared, optimistic, faithful people in whom the miracle of grace was alive and well.

This chapter describes three important understandings about youth: (1) They are persons. (2) They live in a culturally defined context. (3) They are youth in the midst of American life.

Understanding That Youth Are People

It is difficult, if not impossible, to write about how to understand youth. I have a wife whom I do not always understand, a preschooler whom I only occasionally understand, and a Persian cat who is forever beyond my understanding. I don't always understand myself completely. Youth, like all other human beings, are beyond our understanding. Permit me to introduce you to some interesting people I have come to know and love. They are called *youth* at church and *adolescents* in the psychological literature. To understand them you must first understand that they are *people*.

Most of what is true about people is true about youth. What makes them *adolescents* is that they are people at a particular point in life, experiencing particular physiological and psychological changes, living in a particular society which puts particular pressures on them. Underneath all that, they are people. Understanding youth begins with and depends on seeing them as people.

People Are Unique

One characteristic of persons is that they differ from each other. No one fits into a classification or group with precision. Youth, unlike oatmeal, just don't lump together. Some are so giggly you can barely talk with them, others make you cry inside because they never laugh at all. Some are frivolous; others are serious. Some are studious. Some have never read a book; others can't read a book. The most central rule for understanding youth is that *what may be true in general for a group of persons ages twelve to eighteen, may not be true for any one person in that age group.* A book about youth is a book about classifications, generalizations, and characterizations of a large group in our society. Such a book cannot describe each of the Cathy's, David's, Becky's, Chuck's, Maria's, Sarah's, and Carlos' in any particular church. Each youth really needs his or her own book, because youth are each individuals. But so many books would be impossible to write. The best that can be done is to

22

write one volume, but the best one volume can do is deal with a variety of generalities. Youth must always be taken one at a time, each with his or her own hopes, dreams, struggles, and fears.

Youth are all individuals, but they are also persons who share common experiences. School, television, social values, and an onslaught of peddlers and meddlers who earn billions from youth's money create a common atmosphere which youth breathe. While the effect of this atmosphere on any one youth is unknown, the effect it has on the population of youth as a group has been researched and documented. Knowing the group's characteristics and problems can help the leader of youth understand the individual joys and struggles which are encountered by David, Becky, and every other youth.

People Relate to God

Because youth are persons, they have rights and privileges bestowed by God. They possess the privilege to accept the gift of grace offered through God's Son, and the right to refuse it. Because they are persons, youth cannot excuse themselves when they choose to sin or accuse some outside force of causing it. Because they are persons, youth are accountable for the evil they bring into their lives and their world.

Lest this sound too harsh, however, remember that Jesus was born of a teenage mother, blessed the children, and invited people into his kingdom as children. This Jesus understands immaturity, and is incredibly patient with it. Youth are people in the process of maturing. They do not yet know themselves or their world. The gracious God of justice knows the difference between intentional evil and mistakes made because of insufficient knowledge or experience. For those who would understand youth, it will be good to seek a similar wisdom.

People Are People

Youth are people—and to be viewed as such dispels at least one commonly held assumption reflected in the title of this book: *Today's Youth.* That phrase suggests that, in our society rampaging with change, today's youth probably are different from yesterday's or tomorrow's youth. *Youth* seems to need yearly modifiers. Like *cars* and *appliances,* each model is different, and what was true of last year's may not be true of this year's. People—from the Garden where humankind was born to the surface of the moon where they have taken their longest step—have always struggled with under-

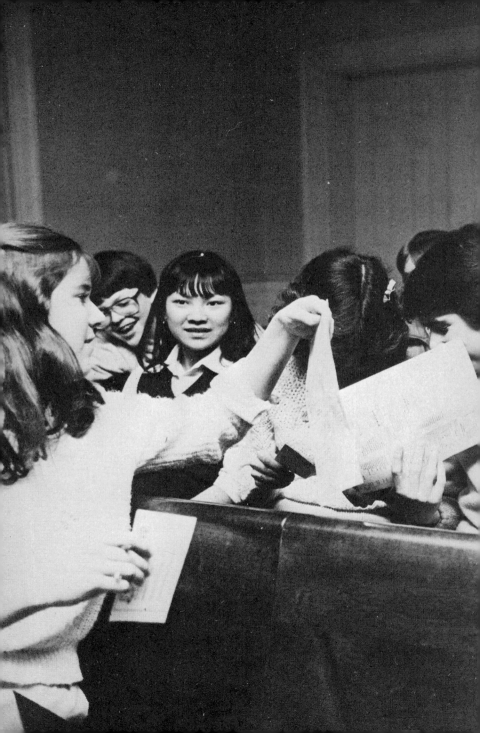

standing themselves. That struggle has led them to search for meaning, to learn to love, to watch children grow, to face death, to battle enemies, and to long for friends and companionship. Being people means that some fundamental experiences of life remain the same.

The world in which youth live has changed from the world I grew up in, and it is likely different from the one you experienced as a fifteen-year-old. Those differences will have a profound effect on "Today's" youth. Youth, however much they may be influenced by the changes in their world, are still persons.

Dealing with broken hearts and family battles; worrying about peers, personality and pimples; deciding what to do when school is out; considering what persons, ideas or institutions deserve one's loyalty—none of these are the exclusive activities of a particular generation of youth. I dealt with them, my parents did, and so will my daughter. There is a continuity in being persons that extends generation after generation. When individuals seek to understand youth, they dare not disregard that continuity.

God Didn't Make Them Adolescents

The title to this section is a statement of truth. God makes persons. Cultures and societies make certain persons into adolescents. While profound physiological changes do occur during the youth years, these characteristics are not the sole cause of the phenomenon known as "adolescence." Another significant cause is the expectations and attitudes which society places on teenagers. The cultural nature of these attitudes requires the title of this chapter to be: "Growing Up *American*."

Among all people, there is a certain similarity as was noted in the preceding section. Also, there are differences caused by growing up in different cultures or in different times within the same culture. Understanding youth begins with the affirmation of their personhood. It continues with an understanding of the cultural influences which place expectations on them and shape their lives.

The Emergence of an American Concept of Adolescence

There was a time, not too long ago, when children went straight from childhood to adulthood. People, in a bygone era, didn't think of a time between puberty and adulthood in which persons had a continued childhood. Not long after they became capable of reproducing, they began to assume the adult roles of work and family.

David Bakan has argued that "The invention or discovery of

adolescence in America was largely in response to the social changes that accompanied America's development in the latter half of the nineteenth and the early twentieth century."[1] As America became increasingly industrial, increasingly urban (even as early as 1900, one-third of Americans lived in cities), and increasingly populated by recent immigrants, the role of teenaged persons began to change. These changes created both an economic and humanitarian reason to treat twelve- to seventeen-year-old persons as older children rather than young adults. Bakan identifies three things American society did which made adolescence an officially recognized period in the life cycle.

First, compulsory public education laws were passed. Education had been considered an issue for parental discretion until state legislative bodies gradually adopted the opinion that education was necessary for a civil society. Society passed laws which removed the decision about whether a child should be educated away from parents. Education was mandated by law, and parents were punishable for keeping children out of school.

Second, child labor laws were passed which made the employment of persons below certain ages illegal. This served to lengthen the period of childhood since fourteen-year-olds, for example, could no longer work full time.

Third, the desire to segregate young lawbreakers from older ones led to the development of the juvenile justice system. Before the turn of the century, a fifteen-year-old lawbreaker could be punished the same way a thirty-five-year-old offender would be. The legislation of juvenile delinquency laws separated youth from older offenders, but it also made it illegal for persons under twenty-one years of age to do some things which persons over twenty-one could do at will (like leaving home without permission, or buying alcohol). These new laws created a different system of judicial record keeping, punishment, and probation for "juveniles."

The enactment of these laws resulted in an officially legislated period in the maturing person's life. This period became known as adolescence. For the first time in American history, persons who were sexually capable of reproduction were, by law, required to attend school whether they wanted to or not; were denied the right to work full time at many jobs, and were guilty of breaking the law by doing things that were lawful for persons over twenty-one. The invention of legal adolescence in American society was pretty well established by the early part of the twentieth century, and began to influence how persons grew up.

For example, it would not have been untypical for a female in 1820 to reach puberty at fifteen, marry at sixteen, have a child at seventeen, and be a grandmother at age thirty-two. A male might have begun working full time in a factory at age thirteen to help support the family into which he was born. By age sixteen or seventeen, he might have been married and supporting his own family. Not all persons married young or began full-time factory work at age fourteen, but many did. No doubt, there was immaturity in those persons. Having a machine to operate, or acres to farm, or a child to care for forced maturity on persons. At the turn of the century, G. Stanley Hall wrote the first American text on adolescent psychology. He said: "Our immigrants have often passed the best years of youth or leave it behind when they reach our shores, and their memories of it are in other lands. No country is so precociously old for its years."[2]

By the 1920's, however, the story was changing. The marrying age, along with inauguration into the work force, was steadily moving upward. Persons were kept from the environments that forced maturity on them, and lived in a period of extended childhood. As adolescents began to be viewed as older children, the expectations society placed on them changed. Those changes altered the process of growing up as Americans.

Cultures Maintain Attitudes About Youth

A culture not only creates a concept like adolescence, it also can maintain attitudes and expectations about youth. Some attitudes vary from culture to culture. In the United States, for example, youth are expected to go to school and not to marry. Many adults view adolescents more as children than adults, and treat them accordingly. Some attitudes transcend cultures and centuries. Adults across generations seem to carry a concern and suspicion regarding the next generation. Socrates, the ancient Greek philosopher, complained: "Children now love luxury; they show disrespect for their parents, chatter before company, gobble up dainties at the table, and tyrannize over their teachers."[3]

The attitudes which people maintain, like the laws a society passes, influence adolescents. If the society expects a fifteen-year-old to be in school, to abstain from sexual relationships, and not to marry, many youth will try hard to live up to the expectations. Others, who want to lash out at their society, have a ready-made way of doing it. If school, church, and family treat sixteen-year-olds like young children, they may act in ways that justify the treatment.

The idea that adolescence is a social invention probably strikes many readers as a bit odd. Yet, it is true. The result is that what is said about understanding youth is highly conditioned by the culture in which they live. Some other cultures treat teenaged persons differently. For example, in 1981, the political turmoil of Iran which led to the dismissal of President Abolhassan Banisadr also led to protests. One group of twelve protesters included an eighteen-year-old girl and eleven other girls, sixteen years of age or younger. All of them were executed for their participation in the nonviolent protest. The Ayatollah Mohammadi Giland explained to reporters: "By the Islamic canon, a nine-year-old girl is mature. So there is no difference for us between a nine-year-old girl and a forty-year-old man."[4] Growing up Iranian is certainly different from growing up American.

Definitions of Adolescence in American Society

Our discussion has already begun to examine the phenomenon of adolescence in America. It is necessary, before going much further, to try to define what is meant by "adolescence" and "youth." A survey of recent texts on adolescent psychology reveals a tendency on the part of many authors to present a variety of definitions because no single one is adequate. Many definitions seek to identify when adolescence begins and when it ends.

It can be argued that adolescence begins with the onset of physical changes which result in puberty. The preceding discussion about the cultural influences means that physiological changes cannot, by themselves, denote the beginning of adolescence. It may be that the beginning of adolescence should be anchored to the onset of the emotional and social overtones of sexual capability—and not just to the emergence of physiological characteristics.

Determining when adolescence ends is even harder than deciding the boundaries that mark its beginning. If adolescence is the time between childhood and the beginnings of adult maturity, then one must first define adult maturity. Maturity, however, is difficult to define. The end of adolescence could be defined as the time when society withdraws the special legal status which the juvenile justice laws have established.

Even though there are problems, there is a need for a usable frame of reference. I propose the following definition: *Adolescence begins with the emergence of the physiological characteristics that result in*

28

puberty. It is accompanied by the social attitudes and expectations that an individual is something other than a child. Adolescence draws to a close as persons begin to assume adult tasks such as work, self-support, marriage, or emotional independence from parents.

Throughout this book, adolescence will be discussed in two periods. *Early adolescence* refers generally to persons in the sixth or seventh through eighth or ninth grades. *Later adolescence* generally refers to the high school years. "Adolescent" and "youth" will be used interchangeably. "Early adolescence" and "younger youth" identify one period; and "later adolescence" or "older youth" describe the second.

Some scholars propose a third stage in the adolescent sequence which includes individuals in their late teen years and early twenties. One twenty-year-old has written: "I view myself as a youth in that I am still going to school, am not married, and am not supporting anyone, which would be some of the characteristics which I think are associated with being an adult."[5] College students frequently fit this description, and sometimes suffer from the problems caused by their being psychologically ready for independence but remaining financially dependent on their parents. This volume will concentrate on middle school/junior high and high school youth.

American Youth in the 80's

American youth are, in one sense, like all youth in all cultures. In another sense, they are unique people who live in a particular culture. They reflect some unique characteristics which deserve attention. Consider some of these characteristics.

Minorities

An increasing percentage of American adolescents will be either Black or Hispanic. Some estimates suggest that by the year 2000, one eighth of the total population will be Black.[6] It is also estimated that by 2000, Hispanic Americans will outnumber Black Americans in the 18 to 21-year-old population.[7] By the year 2000, about 55 percent of 18 to 21-year-olds, will be White, and 45 percent nonwhite. These estimates mean that by the 1990's, 55 percent of the persons 13 to 16-years-old will be white, and 45 percent will be nonwhite.

Adolescence in America is becoming increasingly nonwhite. Because adolescence is at least in part a cultural event, the changing ethnicity of American youth likely will change the character of adolescence in America. This is of particular concern to Southern Baptists who are becoming an increasingly multiethnic denomination.

Nonwhite adolescents might face many problems as they grow up American. Language differences, as well as differences in cultural expectations and family roles can create special difficulties for nonwhite adolescents.

The problem of language is particularly acute for youth growing up in Mexican-American or Puerto Rican families. While Mexican-Spanish is different from Puerto Rican-Spanish, the youth of both minority groups share the problem of one language spoken at home and another language spoken at school.

Minority youth experience American culture differently than white youth do. One Black youth observed: "I remember when I entered school, and I can remember the little books, 'Sally and Jane,' all these in it, and all I would see would be white faces in all my books."[8] Children's books have changed. Few Black first graders in 1983 will have that youth's experience. The development of a positive self-concept or identity, however, can be a major problem for minority youth who feel that others view them with prejudice or disdain. The American world portrayed in television, books, and movies looks less familiar to a Black, Asian, or Hispanic youth than it does to White youth.

One of the confounding problems which minority youth face is that they are more likely to come from poor families. One study has suggested that social class may have more to do with self-concept than race. Both Black and White children who were middle class reflected a more positive self-concept than either Black or White children from lower class families.[9] While this was a study of young children, it might well have some implication about adolescence. Being a poor, minority youth in America may be an overwhelmingly confusing and frustrating experience. With the increasing percentage of American youth who are nonwhite, understanding youth requires that we understand minority youth.

Attitudes

As the decade of the 80's began, a representative sample of over 16,000 high school seniors described themselves in a lengthy survey conducted by the Institute for Social Research at the University of Michigan.[10] Note their findings in the chart.

Survey of High School Seniors

Households where father or male guardian is present   81.7%
Mothers worked during most of youth's growing
up years...   34.0%
Identified as Baptists, largest Protestant group......   21.4%
Attended religious services "about once a week
or more"..   40.7%
Religion was not important......................   10.0%
"Definitely" will graduate from a four-year college. .   31.9%
Will attend graduate or professional school.........   8.8%
"A" students..................................   20.0%
"B" students..................................   53.0%
Less than *B* average............................   27.0%
Worked free or for pay between 11 to 30 hours weekly
during school year...............................   50.0%
Earn incomes of $36.00 plus per week.............   51.0%
Get no allowance................................   41.0%
Go out for fun, one to three nights per week.......   66.4%
Were or had been regular cigarette smokers........   30.0%
Have drunk beer, wine, or liquor..................   93.0%

Defocus on Youth

American society during the last thirty years has been a youth-oriented society. Suburbs grew up in cornfields and hillsides because they would be good places to rear children. School bond issues passed without great resistance in the 1950's and 1960's. The late 1960's brought what many called a "youth culture" and its features (brightly colored clothes, longer hair styles, etc.) were assimilated into American culture as a whole by the 1970's. The appearance, values, and employment of young adults were sought by many. America has been a culture where "young" was good, and old was suspicious, if not bad. Being a youth in a country that valued youth meant that attention was received.

Some indicators during the later 1970's suggested that America is losing its infatuation with youth. The Yankelovich *Monitor* has tracked the trend which it calls "Defocus on Youth." The term "describes the movement *away from* the heavy emphasis that had been placed on the values, needs, and importance of youth in our society."[11] For example, 22 percent of the American population sampled in 1975 saw men under twenty-five years of age as the fashion trend setters. In 1980, 16 percent of the American population sampled looked to men in the same age bracket for fashion trends. Thirty-four percent of the population in 1975 looked to persons under twenty-five years of age as the trend setters in hair fashion. That percentage was reduced to 27 percent in 1980. These data suggest that the persons in American society are apparently idealizing the young slightly less than they did in the early 1970's, and are looking to them as trend setters less than they once did.

For youth growing up in the 80's, there likely will be less societal recognition. When the world is youth oriented, an individual is special just because he or she is young. When the society becomes less youth oriented, youth will be viewed as less special.

Summary and Conclusion

Adolescence is a time of poetry, despair, hopes, dreams, moods, love, and hate. Adolescence is something that happens partly because of biological forces. Other cultural forces, however, determine the time and kind of youth years. The biological forces will always create the same tensions, but the tensions and concerns created by social expectations may shift from culture to culture.

To grow up American is something special. What is true for American adolescents likely will be true in other societies similar to the United States. What is true for American youth, however, may not be true for all youth.

Because most of the adults reading this book are probably American born, and probably under sixty years of age, their experiences of adolescence bear a great deal of similarity to the experiences youth in the 80's likely will encounter.

More than a difference between younger youth and older ones there is a great uniqueness in each youth. Each is a person. Each is a unique gift the Creator God has fashioned for this world. Each is worth celebration. Each youth—the smart, handsome one and the goofy, pimply one—is loved by God, and surely should be loved by others. Understanding youth begins by taking seriously their individuality.

Personal Learning Activities

Listed below are concerns of youth. Some of them always have been and likely will be a part of every youth's experience. To the left of each, write an *A* if it is a concern of every generation and *T* if it is a unique concern of today's youth.

_A_ Wanting acceptance by peers

_A_ Desires conflicting with parents'

_A_ Attending a middle school

_A_ Church friends going to different schools

_A_ Deciding what to do after high school

_T_ Having attended two or more elementary schools

_A_ Developing a personal faith

_T_ Going to school/church with persons of various ethnic groups

_A_ Relating to persons of the opposite sex

_T_ Deciding what to do when offered drugs/alcohol

_T_ Living with only one parent

34

How would you define the beginning and end of adolescence?

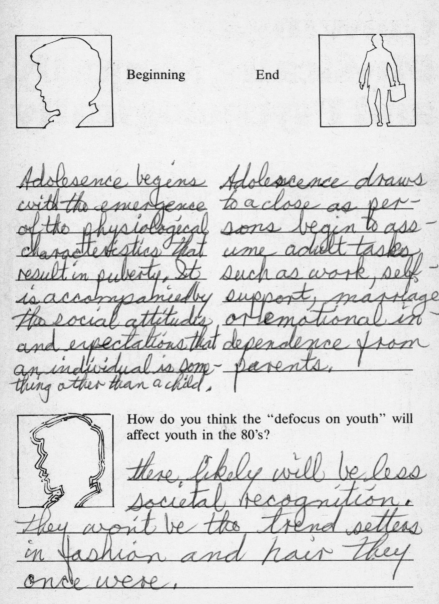

Beginning   End

Adolesence begins with the emergence of the physiological characteristics that result in puberty. It is accompanied by the social attitudes and expectations that an individual is something other than a child.

Adolescence draws to a close as persons begin to assume adult tasks such as work, self-support, marriage, or emotional independence from parents.

How do you think the "defocus on youth" will affect youth in the 80's?

there likely will be less societal recognition. they won't be the trend setters in fashion and hair they once were.

35

Growing Up Physically, Mentally, and Psychologically

R.R. Hester

3

Growing Up Physically, Mentally, and Psychologically

"Well, like I go to Waggoner, you know, some parts are separated from the high school students, but sometimes you see the high school students. And it's sort of scary because, I mean, all these big, old, tall, huge guys walking down the hall, you get run over, and it's sort of scary."

—Middle School Youth

When giants are in the land, it *is* scary. It *is* scary, when friends' bodies are changing, and yours isn't. It *is* scary, when the body to which you have grown dependably accustomed begins to change. Legs cover different distances. Arms move about, hopelessly out of control. Voices crack. Bodies produce new odors. Hair grows in new places.

It *is* scary, when all of a sudden, puberty occurs, like an unknown prowler creeping over the body bringing new shapes and aches. A permanent change invades. Bodies will never return to the proportions of childhood.

Understanding youth requires some understanding of the perva-

38

sive body changes which occur during the youth years. Youth also experience changes in their ability to think, their emotions, and personality. These changes also require the attention of leaders of youth.

The first three years of life are the only period where bodily, emotional, and intellectual changes are as great as they are in adolescence. Never again will the natural process of human development bring such overwhelming and fundamental change in such a short period of time. This chapter describes some of these many changes.

Physical Changes

The hypothalamus is a tiny gland at the base of the brain which causes a revolution of major proportions in the lives of older elementary school children. This regulatory center in the brain grows sufficiently mature in older childhood to activate the pituitary gland. This gland secretes gonadotropic hormones which stimulate the increased production of estrogens (the feminizing hormones) and androgens (the masculinizing hormones). These hormones and the body's complex feedback systems cause the physical and physiological changes that occur during adolescence. *(Fortunately, youth do not need to know about these hormones for them to be effective, nor do youth leaders need to be able to pronounce their names in order to be competent guides and helpers for youth!)*

For males and females, some of the bodily changes are similar. Others distinguish and emphasize the physical uniquenesses of the two sexes.

Kinds of Physical Changes

One common change is the "growth spurt." Through most of the school-age years individuals experience gradual and uniform growth. With the onset of puberty, however, the rate of growth accelerates, for both males and females. Females usually have their greatest increase in height about two years before males do. Height may increase from four to twelve inches for boys during the growth spurt, somewhat less for girls. The average increase in height for boys during the growth spurt is four inches per year.[1] The growth spurt brings more than a new quantity of growth. It causes different parts of the body to grow at different rates. "The head, hands, and feet reach adult size first. In turn, the arms and legs grow faster than trunk length, which is completed last."[2] The unevenness of growth causes many youth to be awkward or clumsy.

The growth spurt is evident to parents in another way. Parents who have spent the first eleven years trying to get their child to eat begin wondering if they can pay the food bill! *Table 1*[3] shows the recommended daily caloric needs for adolescents. They eat a lot, and need it.

TABLE 1
Dietary Recommendations for Adolescents

	Age	Weight	Height	Calories
Males	11-14	97	5'3"	2800
	15-18	134	5'9"	3000
Females	11-14	97	5'2"	2100
	15-18	119	5'5"	2100

Some bodily changes are unique to males while others are unique to females. These changes transform similar appearances of boys and girls of middle childhood into different appearances of men and women in adulthood. Males experience an increase in the size of genitals, the growth of pubic and body hair, an increase in the length of the vocal chords, development of a beard, the ability to reproduce sexually, and an increased musculature. Each of these changes emphasizes the maleness of males and distinguishes them from females. Females experience an increase in the size of genitals, the budding and development of breasts, the appearance of pubic hair, enlargement of hips and pelvic region, menarche (first period) and subsequent regular ovulation. All of these changes accentuate an adolescent girl's femaleness.

One of the interesting things happening to American youth is called "the secular trend." Children are growing up sooner. According to some records, individuals in 1900 achieved their maximal height during their mid-twenties. In the middle of the 1970's, statistics indicated that girls attained maximal height at age sixteen or seventeen, and boys at eighteen or nineteen. Adolescent girls in the United States have been experiencing menarche (first menstrual period) at earlier and earlier ages, many of them between eleven and thirteen years of age. Children *age* growing up *faster*. Also they are growing up *more*. Average weight and height of successive American generations has been increasing.

The reason for the "secular trend" may be the overall improvement in nutrition which Americans have experienced over the last century. Better prenatal care and nutrition for expectant mothers and better food and nutrition during growing-up years have contributed to the effect. Some evidence indicates that the "secular trend" is diminishing, and that the age at which puberty occurs is stabilizing.

Influence of Physical Changes

The physical forms youth develop have profound influences both on the ways others view them and the ways they view themselves. Pretty girls are more likely to receive help from strangers, to say nothing of invitations for dates. Females who view themselves as unattractive, or are seen that way by peers, have greater difficulty feeling worthwhile and self-confident. Late maturing youth are likely to be influenced by their childlike appearance in the midst of friends who look more like adults, while early maturers are more likely to be elected to leadership positions by peers. Early maturing males are more likely to participate in athletic events, which frequently enhance their prestige with other youth. Generally, early maturing males experience more advantages than early maturing females do.[4]

Because physical changes are so obvious to others, they provide an easy means for stereotyping. Athletic looking males are expected to be athletic; "voluptuous" looking females are expected to be sexy; "studious" looking youth are expected to be brainy. Judgments based on appearance are judgments over which youth have little control, and may be particularly punitive in the lives of many.

Physical changes also influence moods and emotions in two ways. First, the hormones that cause the development of adult physical characteristics also influence moods. Anyone who lives or works with early adolescents can testify to sudden mood changes, extremes in moods, and moodiness. While these characteristics are not true of all youth, they are true for many. The mood fluctuations are caused, at least in part, by the dramatic increase in hormone levels. For example, a girl of 12 to 14 years will have 20 times the amount of estrogen as she had during childhood years.[5]

Second, youth's reaction to their physical changes and the reactions others have to them influence moods. Some youth fear that something is wrong because they grew so much or so little. Other youth are depressed because some features developed in ways they

42

think other people consider as ugly or undesirable.

Youth Ministry and Physical Changes

Why all this material about hormones and growth spurts in a book for Sunday School teachers and other leaders of youth? Because part of their ministry arises out of the problems physical changes bring. Leaders need to be aware of the changes and the ministry they can provide.

For example, adolescent physical development produces both mature sexual characteristics and the heightening of a sexual drive. New desires exist, and they require youth to rethink their values and learn to abide by them.

Physical changes make some youth feel unlovable. They think themselves to be ugly, unacceptable people. But the gospel is good news that all people are loved—even the people who do not love themselves *(John 3:16)*. Some youth need to be reminded that God loves them as do others.

Physical changes make the world seem less predictable and dependable than it once was. The call to faith, the love of Christ, and the integrity of scriptural truth are predictable and dependable. Youth need to be encouraged to continue to believe these long-term truths in the midst of constantly changing short-term feelings.

Physical changes create a rash of anxieties, fears, feelings of guilt and frustration, worry and pride. Youth leaders can help youth with each of these feelings, and acquaint them with the resources of the Christian faith for dealing with human fears, anxieties, and frustrations.

Above all, leaders of youth minister as they love and accept youth—regardless of a youth's appearance, athletic ability, or physical prowess.

Intellectual Changes

Bodies are not the only things which change in adolescence. The person's ability to think also changes. *(Now, parents might question this assertion, since they frequently find themselves asking their kids: Why don't you think before you . . . ?)* But, cognitive (thinking) ability does undergo significant change during adolescence. That change is not evidenced by a great increase in intelligence. Individuals, however, do show a gradual increase in the scores they obtain on IQ tests through childhood and youth years. The most pronounced cognitive changes which occur in youth relate to the *kind* of thinking

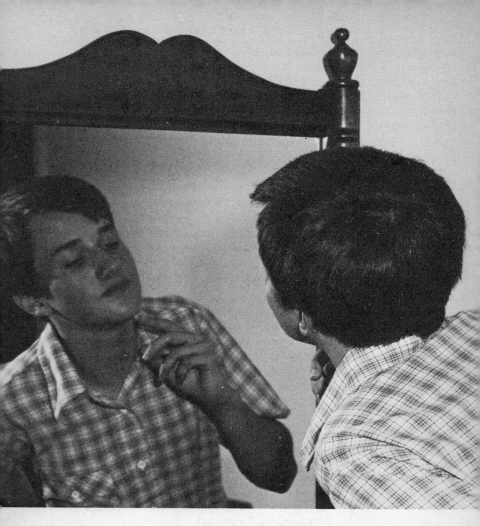

youth can do. (Intelligence, measured by IQ, is an indicator of the amount of mental ability.)

Jean Piaget, a Swiss psychologist who died in 1980, has had a profound influence on understanding the nature of thinking and how it grows. He argued that the differences in thinking ability between a preschooler, school-age child, and youth are not just differences in learning and the amount of intellectual capacity. Rather, he argued that thinking develops through a series of stages. Each new stage brings a different way of thinking which is an improvement on the earlier one. There are four major stages, and individuals mature through three of these during preschool and elementary school years. Adolescence is marked by passage into the fourth or formal operational stage. Formal operational thought is adult-like and provides youth with thinking abilities they have never had earlier.[6] Chief among these is the ability to think in abstractions. Earlier, the child was locked into thinking in concrete terms. He or she could understand things that could be seen or touched, but could not deal readily with ideas or concepts. The development of formal operational thought permits adolescents to think about their world apart from its immediate, concrete parts. It gives them the ability to formulate hypotheses, to perceive relationships, to think about what they are experiencing, to build theories. Scientific studies of school-age children clearly indicate that these abilities don't exist prior to twelve to fourteen years of age.

One writer has described the kind of change in thinking which youth experience. Preadolescents "can imagine . . . the teacher and the school, but not education; the policeman and the judge and the jail, but not the law; the public official but not the government."[7] Adolescence, however, brings the kind of logical thought which enables youth to begin thinking about education, law, and government, as well as theological realities, such as love, grace, and justice.

The new cognitive ability also allows youth to begin thinking about the future and past as well as the present, and to begin thinking of principles that can guide their decision making.

The change in cognitive ability has a great impact on religious thinking and moral development. It requires serious attention in the ministry churches share with youth. Those issues will be highlighted in the chapter "Growing Up and Faith Formation."

Psychological Development

The development of the ability to think logically and abstractly affects another area of youths' lives: their emotions and psychological development.[8] Emotions are a visible part of adolescence, and they influence both the youth and the people who live or work with them. Understanding youth includes understanding psychological and emotional development during adolescence.

Quest for Identity

Erik Erikson has been a molding force in the way developmental psychologists view emotional growth during adolescence. He has argued from case history evidence that the crucial factor in emotional development is the youth's struggle with his or her identity—or lack of it. It is a struggle to become a whole person.

> Young people must become whole people in their own right, and this during a developmental stage characterized by a diversity of changes in physical growth, genital maturation, and social awareness. The wholeness to be achieved at this stage I have called a *sense of inner identity.*[9]

The struggle with identity is not the first one encountered in life. Erikson has seen human development as a series of "crises" (by which he means turning points, times of heightened potential and vulnerability). An individual has already encountered four of these developmental turning points by the time she/he reaches adolescence.

The crisis of adolescence, according to Erikson, is "Identity *versus* Identity Confusion." The positive outcome is an inner sense of identity in which youth have an accurate sense of who they are. The potential negative outcome is that youth never know who they are and develop unrealistic or distorted images of themselves. This confused identity may be reflected in an overidentification with some individual or peer group, or cause a youth to act like someone else instead of being him/herself.

Identity comes from many different sources. One is the childhood histories youth bring to adolescence and the sense of the future they may have. A second is the perspective youth have of themselves and how they think others view them. A third source includes youths' families, ethnic identification, and culture.[10] These tell youth: "You are white." "You are minority." "You are the child your parents love best." "You are the child your parents love least."

On one hand, youth can just accept all the signals which history, abilities, family, peers, and culture give them about their identity. But the signals are frequently conflicting, and if taken at face value, can contribute to a sense of inner confusion. On the other hand, youth can be synthesizers and organizers of all this information, and develop a realistic sense of who they are, what they are like, and what they can do.

Youth are guided in their process of forming identity in several ways. The choosing of occupation gives some concrete data for youth to use in claiming identity. Since American society requires a great deal of schooling for many occupations, occupational identity may come in the form of being in the precollege or the vocational tracks in high school.[11] Another way youth explore their identity is by falling in and out of love. Being someone's boyfriend or girl friend can help them discover characteristics about themselves. Youth may rebel against the society and adult world because they are not sure who they are as individuals.[12] Rebellion can be in the form of youth thinking themselves either noble in an evil society or indulgent in an artificially restrictive one. Either form is rebellion, and rebellion may occur because youth are trying to discover who they really are.

Still another method youth may use to help with the struggle of identity is a kind of moratorium. Erikson explains that "A moratorium is a period of delay granted to somebody who is not ready to meet an obligation,"[13] and applies the concept to human development.

> By psychosocial moratorium, then, we mean a delay of adult commitments, and yet it is not only a delay. It is a period that is characterized by a selective permissiveness on the part of society and of provocative playfulness on the part of youth.[14]

The moratorium is Erikson's way of describing what others sometimes call "sowing wild oats." He contends that this kind of behavior is not just a youth's disregard for morality. It grows from the individual's fundamental problem with his or her identity.

We have explored Erikson's understanding of emotional development because it has good supporting evidence, has a wide base of acceptance among other theorists, and seems to fit well with some commonsense experiences with youth. There are other arguments as to what are the most important influences in adolescent emotional development. The struggle with identity, however, seems to be a central struggle for many American youth. Possibly, the freedom of choice American society grants to individuals causes a greater need to develop a sense of identity. In societies where an individual's marriageability, occupation, and status are all determined by birth, identity may be less a problem for adolescents. Whatever the cause, the struggle for identity seems to be a major issue in American adolescence, if not American society as a whole.

47

Adolescent Emotions

In addition to the struggle of identity, adolescence also is a period of life when emotions are noticeable. Love, anger, hate, depression, exhilaration—all in large doses—can occur in a single day's experience. G. Stanley Hall has characterized adolescent development as a period of extreme "storm and stress." There are stormy times with friends and family, and stormy times when youth are off by themselves. Why are there such intense emotional times?

One reason for youthful emotionality is the presence of new amounts of hormones in adolescent bodies. While some of the moody behavior may be learned from a society which teaches youth that hormones affect moods, there is evidence that the hormones do impact emotions. Another reason for youth to be so emotional is that rapidly changing bodies influence how youth feel about themselves. They frequently feel less positively about themselves as bodies are changing, and the result is moodiness and mood extremes.

In addition to biological and physical influences, youth also experience stresses which affect emotions. Peter Blos has argued that adolescence is a time when the individual is torn between the security of dependency and the desire to become independent.[15] In one moment, the youth is a child seeking security and sanctuary in the family. In the next moment, the youth is annoyed by the demands of family life and is wishing to be off on his or her own. These ambivalent feelings not only keep parents frustrated and on the defensive, but also they cause confusion and exaggerated emotional expressions in youth.

Two other adolescent tendencies have been interpreted as causing strong emotions. Youth tend to be very self-conscious. "Adolescents are extremely conscious not only of their bodies but also of their minds. They are often aware of a sharp discrepancy between the selves they are and the selves that they wish to become—that is, their ideal self."[16] The result of this self-consciousness can be embarrassment, hurt, or shame. Youth also have the tendency to view the world in idealistic ways. "The youthful capacity for idealism often leads adolescents to regard family, religion, and society in general in a derogatory manner because of the wide contrast between the ideal and the real."[17] The effect can be a lack of compassion, lashing out in anger, feelings of depression, or a mixture of other emotions that accompany the shattering of an ideal.

When people think of youthful emotions, they often think of the exaggerations, the intensity, and the negative traits. Also, there are

positive emotions which develop during adolescence. Youth continue to learn how to love and care for people, and their love takes on a more altruistic (unselfish) nature. Learning to love family members, friends, and an individual of the opposite sex; learning that love is different from infatuation, and that love and sex are not the same thing—all of these are important parts of healthy, emotional development in youth. Learning to love and care for others is something to be celebrated and nurtured by the community of faith.

Summary

Sketching physical, intellectual, and emotional changes during adolescence is always dangerous. Every youth is first of all a person, and people are different. What is true of youth in general is not necessarily true of any particular youth.

All youth experience profound physical and physiological changes. All youth, however, do not respond to the changes in the same way. Some youth don't seem to be bothered by what's going on, others seem to be on a perennial teeter-totter (seesaw) with hourly ups and downs. Many youth grow up without too much emotional exaggeration. They don't rebel or drop out. It is important not to confuse the *descriptions* of what happens to many youth with a *prescription* of what should happen. Youth don't need to rebel, or declare a moratorium, or act moody, or be cynical to be healthy. For some youth, growing up is a difficult, almost disastrous process. For others, it is the enjoyable encounter of life.

Personal Learning Activities

Beside each of the youth listed below, write a statement describing something an adult can do or give to the youth that will affirm his/her personal worth.

A short seventh grade boy _____

_____

The first girl in the group to begin monthly periods _____

_____

A fat, self-conscious eighth grade girl _____

_____

A quiet, studious fourteen-year-old boy_____

_____

Enthusiastic youth who is always present at church activities

_____

50

Piaget has identified adolescence as the stage of
_____ thinking. What abilities
does this kind of thinking involve? _____

How does knowing that youth are capable of ab-
stract thought provide a challenge for
church leaders of youth? _____
parents? _____

What are three sources of identity named by
Erikson?
1.

2.

3.

Think of a youth you know. How is he or she struggling to find his/her
identity? Write a description of the youth and the struggle.

Who am I? Who am I?

Growing Up with Families

R.R. HESTER

4

Growing Up with Families

From a Discussion with a High School Youth Group

LEADER: Describe, for me, the ideal mother and father.

YOUTH: Somebody with no mouth!

YOUTH: They would wear earplugs.

YOUTH: Yeah, and dark glasses—so you couldn't see their eyes.

LEADER: Any other, more serious, responses?

YOUTH: Somebody who at least remembered what it was like to be a teenager.

YOUTH: My parents set a standard at our house that you could date when you turn sixteen. Well, I turned sixteen in February, and they said I could date, but couldn't have the car.

They seem to forget about the times when they were our age. The things we want to do now they wanted to do then.

LEADER: What else? What makes a good parent?

YOUTH: I think it's better when parents are young. They understand better.

YOUTH: They should give us a chance to try out stuff.

YOUTH: They should trust us enough to give us the benefit of the doubt that we know when to stop.

LEADER: Many of you in this conversation have talked about problems you have with your parents. How many of you, despite this conversation feel that your relationship with your parents is more good than bad?

(About 18 of 20 youth present raised their hands.)

YOUTH: I've come to the realization in the past year or so that my parents try to be pretty good. There are certain things here and there that they lose all reason about and become illogical and arbitrary, but there's not really a whole lot you can do about that.

Parents have a public relations problem with youth. Almost any youth group can get a conversation going concerning the problems they have with parents. At first hearing, it sounds as if youth come to church from torture chambers where parents stalk around in fits of unreasonableness. If the conversation goes long enough, however, or the questions get worded the right way, a majority of church youth will admit to getting along well with their parents. This consistent paradox—"My parents are terrible, but we get along OK"—is a typical pattern.

Families are important for youth. They nurture love and self-awareness. They also become the territory for some major battles, frustrations, and anguish. Families are blessing and curse, the givers of both joy and pain.

Parents are important people in the lives of youth. Psychologist John Conger has concluded:

> An impressive body of research and clinical investigation makes it clear that the single most important influence in helping or hindering the average adolescent to cope with the developmental demands of adolescence in today's world is his or her parents."[1]

Youth are not always aware of just how important parents are, and parents frequently feel as though they have no real influence on their

55

adolescents. Neither the awareness of the youth nor the perception of the parents is accurate. Parents are important.

Brothers and sisters are important, too. They provide opportunity to deal with conflict and competition. Also, a brother or sister provides understanding, a source of motivation, and a model to lead younger brothers or sisters through the adolescent maze.

Many of today's youth live with only one parent. Thus, they are deprived of daily interaction with the other parent and the influences that parent might offer. The single parent is overburdened with work responsibilities and management of the home. In such circumstances, the youth assumes adult roles and responsibilities, sometimes before he or she is ready.

Parents, brothers, and sisters comprise an influential arena in which most youth grow up. It is an arena that can look like a battleground at one time and a playground at another. It is the scene of many of life's extremes: dearest warmth, fiercest struggles, deepest love, bitterest rivalry. This chapter deals with adolescent's relationship with their families.

Youth and Family

"You wouldn't believe what goes on in our family." At first, you might suppose a youth uttering that line was divulging some family secret. When pushed, many youth explain comments like that one by talking about experiences which almost every family has. A common thread of family experience exists in the midst of all that is unique. This section explores a few of these typical aspects of family life.

Influence of Family

As children become adolescents, the role of family in their life changes. For preschool children, family was virtually the only world they knew. Their world grew larger during elementary school years when schoolteachers and classmates took some of the time that once was spent with family. By adolescence, the family has changed from being the center of the individual's universe to being one of many arenas in which life is lived.

While the shift does not take away the vital importance of family, it does change the way the family exerts its influence. The family provides the environment in which the infant and young child can be dependent. The family's role becomes more complex when the dependent child grows into an adolescent. The family must, on one

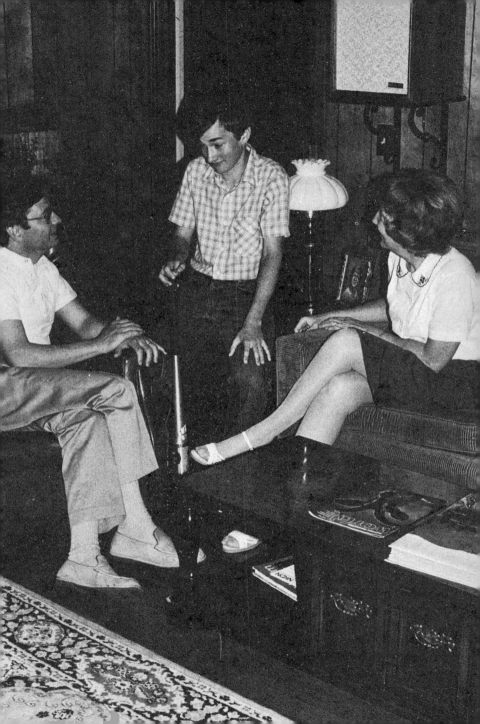

hand, cater to a youth's continuing dependency needs. On the other hand, it must nurture and instruct the youth to a growing sense of independence. The family's role changes from a single emphasis (providing a secure environment for a dependent child) to a conflicting double emphasis (accommodating dependency while pushing independence).

Children view parents differently in their adolescent years than they did during elementary school years. The elementary child typically construes parents as the authority in his or her life. In an argument, elementary age children are likely to seek out an adult as the arbitrator and authority. Youth, however, are more likely to seek out significant friends and peers as authorities. Parents' tastes in clothes, music, or hairstyles are not nearly as authoritative as the tastes of peers. The tendency to view peers as authorities does not hold true for every area of life, but it is true for many. Parents who have grown accustomed to being seen as authorities by their young children sometimes are bewildered by the shift they sense when their children become adolescents.

Roles and Rôle Influences

The family is an environment which interprets the role of males and females to children, and frequently assigns functional roles to family members which are not related to gender. "Mother" and "father" or "husband" and "wife" are terms that come to have meaning based on the youth's understanding of sex roles. Sex roles help youth identify the meaning of their maleness or femaleness. In addition to sex roles, many youth fill a particular role in the family. For example, a youth may become the family socializer, or the "smart one." The roles youth fill in their family may influence the roles they adopt as adults.

Sex Roles. Robert Havighurst theorizes that one of the major tasks of adolescents is to achieve a masculine or feminine role. He has written, "Since the masculine and feminine roles are different in our society, a boy has to accept the idea of becoming a man and a girl has to accept the idea of becoming a woman."[2] Males must decide what it is to be a man, and then set out on a course to become one. Females must decide what it is to be a woman, and pursue that vision. American girls, I think, have a greater difficulty deciding on their sex role. The range of roles is far greater for females than males. For example, most males will not feel free to decide between having a career or being a house husband with wives who are principal wage earners. Some females do have the opportunity for such a choice.

The family exerts a great deal of influence on the sex role identification of youth. Sometimes, the influence may come as a prescription of what masculine or feminine should mean. At other times, the influence may be by disapproval of the role a youth expresses. Always, the influence comes from youth observing parents who exhibit different concepts of masculine and feminine as they live their lives.

Family Roles. Brothers and sisters take on family roles. Some research indicates that a child's age and sex as well as his/her order of birth will influence the roles the family ascribes to him or her. Adolescent males, for example, in families with only boys have a tendency to adopt traditional "masculine" characteristics, such as independence and dominance. Adolescent females in families with only girls tend to express traditional "feminine" qualities. Other evidence suggests that each child fills a particular role in a family, especially in larger families. One child, for example, fills a role in which he or she is a supervisor of other children. Another child might fill the role of the sociable organizer of family fun and laughter. Sometimes, the role is assigned by siblings or parents; other times, it seems to be a role a child assumes. In either event, family roles appear to be a normative influence on youth.

Common Occurrences

People are unique, and because families are comprised of people, they can be nothing other than unique. What is true of one family is not necessarily true of another. Many families, however, do experience some or all of the following feelings.

Conflict. Individuals sometimes think of conflict as a disease that only a few infected families have, but conflict is a common occurrence. Adolescent children are moving toward independence; and many decide that parental restrictions are increasingly oppressive or restrictive. The result is conflict between youth and parents. Brothers and sisters experience conflict with each other. While it probably started in the sandbox or the playpen, the conflict can become more intense as adolescents clash in opposition.

In families with adolescents, a number of forces which can cause conflict are at work. Youth may feel insecure and act defensively. Parents may feel frustrated because their influence seems to be lessening and they fear their children will abandon parental values and dreams. Because conflict is common the sting or hurt is not taken away from its occurrence. Families need to be aware that they are not alone in their hurts.

Fragmentation. As family becomes one more of many arenas in a youth's life instead of the primary one, feelings of fragmentation emerge. Family dinners seem to be a thing of the past. Family outings are difficult to schedule. Most youth have friends outside the home who dominate their time and leisure. Parents react to these changes with concern: "Our family just isn't together the way we used to be." "It seems that we never have time to talk as a family. What's wrong with us?" Youth react with feelings of resentment and exclaim: "Oh, boy. A night at home with the family; I can hardly stand the excitement. My parents are always bugging me about staying home. I can't stand my little sister. My parents really have a weird idea of what a good time is!"

While parents worry that their family has somehow failed, and youth complain that home is a bleak place to spend free time, both should be aware that they are encountering typical experiences of families with adolescents. Christians should take family responsibility seriously, and seek to have good families. As children become adolescents, Christian parents need not interpret the typical changes in family life as evidence of sin or failure.

Concerns. Wherever there is love, there will be concerns. The amount of love varies from one family to another. Where love is, however, concerns and worries frequently creep around. Parents grow concerned as they realize they cannot protect an adolescent from some dangers the way they could when that youth was a preschooler. Youth express concerns about the degree of closeness they feel with their families. In a nationwide survey of church youth, about 20 percent responded that they are "very much" or "quite bothered" that "we are not close as family members."[3] About one fifth of church youth express concern that their fathers are not as interested in them as they would like. Concern about the stability of the home flourishes when youth sense that mother and father are seriously at odds with each other.

Contentment. While the data are not available for American youth as a whole, the majority of American church youth (including Southern Baptists) are content with their families. Two thirds feel that their parents get along fairly well; and over half express contentment with the degree of closeness family members have with one another.

While the surface opinions youth express about family are sometimes discouraging, most youth—in the midst of the conflict, fragmentation, role expectations, and concerns—have a sense of confidence and contentment about their families.

Youth and Parents

No mouth, earplugs, and dark glasses: those are the characteristics the youth in our discussion decided would make for perfect parents. It was kind of them, I thought, to decide on earplugs and dark glasses. They could have declared that parents should have neither hearing nor vision. When I asked why they wanted parents to have dark glasses, the youth said that they didn't mind so much what parents saw; they just didn't want to have to look parents in the eyes! "Bright kids," I thought to myself. Although all this conversation was part of the bright remark prelude which frequently precedes a serious conversation among youth, it still revealed something.

They wanted the parents to see—that's the lingering feeling of dependence, wanting to be watched over and parented. They, however, didn't want to have to look into parent's eyes—that's the knowledge that independence sometimes puts youth and their parents on a collision course. The dependence-independence tension is one of many dynamics that define the youth-parent relationship. We will consider two questions as a way of exploring that relationship. What makes good parents? What is appropriate discipline for adolescents?

What Makes Good Parents?

People are what make good parents. Parenthood is not a child-rearing machine which, if well oiled and tuned, will bring children up successfully. Parenthood is people who have insight and blindspots, joys and depressions, abilities and inabilities. It is males and females who, by God's gift, have children to usher into the human family. There are no secret formulas which will assure successful parenting. There is no list of qualities which guarantee parental success. Research does suggest some characteristics that contribute to positive growth for adolescents. Psychologist John Conger summarizes three of these characteristics.

Love and Trust. Adolescents need "loving, caring parents whom they can trust and in whom they can have confidence . . . Without clear manifestations of parental love, the child or adolescent has little chance of developing self-esteem, constructive and rewarding relationships with others, and a confident sense of his or her own identity."[4] The research only confirms what was said in the discussion reported at the beginning of this chapter: "They should trust us," the youth said. A loving relationship requires both trust toward the youth and the trustability of the parent. Merton Strommen's investigation of church youth showed that feelings of mistrust are a potent factor in family conflict. When youth feel parents don't trust them, research shows that family disunity is nineteen times more likely than the simple fact of a divorce.[5]

Youth sometimes do things that tear away at parents' trust. That is a reality that must be dealt with. Parents, however, can contribute to a youth's destructive behavior by untrusting and pessimistic attitudes. Love and trust are fundamental gifts which parents should give their children. Conger has noted: "Parental hostility, rejection, or neglect consistently occur more often than acceptance, love, and trust in the backgrounds of children with a very wide variety of problems."[6]

Love and trust not only are necessities of life for most children, but also they are fundamental teachings of the Scriptures. To grow up in families without love and trust is to be exposed to the ravages of sin—which so frequently is the breeding place for behavior that becomes sinful.

Controlled Freedom. Another characteristic which makes good parents is a balance between control and freedom. Youth experience problems *both* when there is too much control *and* when there is too much freedom. Good parenting involves finding the appropriate balance.

Christian parents sometimes equate strict parenting with Christian parenting. That view is not necessarily biblical. The story of the loving father and the prodigal son (Luke 15:11-32) is a parable about a father who knew when to give freedom. God relates to men and women as father, and a gift he gives in that relationship is freedom. People are not coerced into righteousness. They are invited to it, empowered to live it, and shown why it is a "more excellent way." The Father God of the Bible, however, grants freedom and the right to choose—even though people do not always choose best.

Freedom is not the only gift God gives his children. "Those whom I love, I reprove and chasten; so be zealous and repent" (Rev. 3:19, RSV). Those are the words of the Amen, the True Witness to the church at Laodicea. They speak about another gift God the Father gives: the gift of discipline or control. One of the goals of parenting is to help youth learn to discipline themselves (that is, to be self-

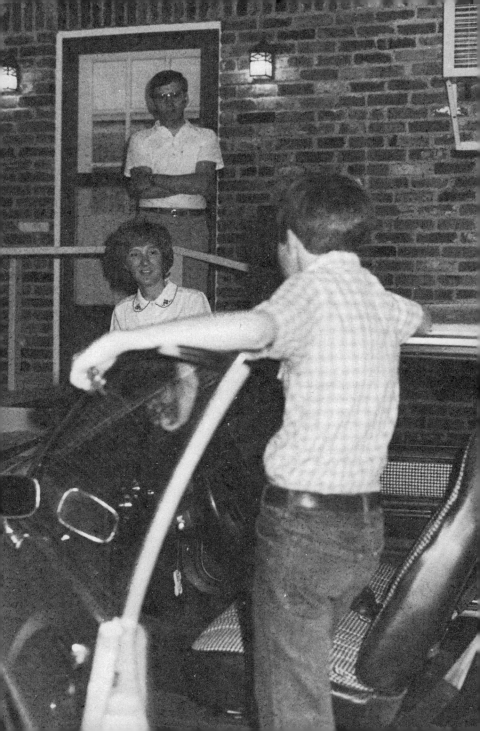

disciplined). Parents need to provide necessary discipline both until self-discipline emerges and to help it form. Discipline—of the right kind in the right amount—is necessary for youth. Good parenting, as reflected in the parenting God gives his children, seeks an appropriate balance of freedom and control.

Authoritative Caring. Youth need parents to be parents, not older brothers and sisters. They need the authority of parental love. That doesn't mean that parents should be authoritarian or autocratic. In fact, many authors use the word *authoritative* to distinguish from *authoritarian.* Authoritative and caring parents take stands with youth when stands must be taken. They are willing to hear their children. They recognize the need for give-and-take, but know where the buck stops. They are willing to say *no* or *yes* and accept their responsibility as parents. They are parents who realize that their job is to help youth learn how to live life on their own.

The Scriptures affirm the authoritative concept of parenting in passages such as Ephesians 6:1 which admonishes children to obey their parents. The Scriptures, however, do not give parents permission to be authoritarian; they can't do anything they want simply because they are parents. The same passage admonishes fathers "do not provoke your children to anger, but bring them up in the discipline and instruction of the Lord" (Eph. 6:4, RSV). The confusion of Christian discipleship and autocratic discipline is a dangerous one which Christian parents and youth workers must avoid. The affirmation of Scripture is a call to parental responsibility. The integrity of that scriptural call is reflected in some recent research which led John Conger to conclude:

> In several recent studies of middle-class adolescents, high-risk drug use and other forms of socially deviant behavior were found to occur most frequently among the children of parents who outwardly expressed such values as individuality, self-understanding, and the need for equalitarianism within the family, *but actually used these proclaimed values to avoid assuming parental responsibility.*[7]

Parents need to assume the responsibility of being parents. To do that, they must have authority. The attraction of many Christians to authoritarianism and its emphasis on parental power assertion is more an invention of the Evil One than an outgrowth of true discipleship. The Scriptures seldom talk in terms of who has power over whom. Rather, people are called to accept responsibility, love, and care, and live under the mandate of mutual submission. (See Eph. 5:21.)

Open Communication. Another characteristic which contributes to good parenting is constant communication. Merton Strommen found that the 25 percent of church youth who reported the most positive feelings about their families said they felt free to discuss their problems with their mothers.[8] In the conversation reported at the beginning of this chapter, some youth talked about wanting parents who would understand. Communication and understanding are cousins, if not brothers and sisters. Communication depends on the presence of love and trust. It also depends on parents' commitment to work at communication: learning to listen to youth; willing to take the time to talk with youth who frequently find it difficult to put into words feelings they don't understand.

Communication is not a cure-all for family aches. If, however youth or parents can talk to each other, communication can provide some healing. The importance of communication is not just something which psychologists recently observed. It is a crucial ingredient in the disciple's life. Prayer is communication between God and individuals. Scripture is replete with references which affirm the central importance of prayer (for example, "Pray without ceasing"—1 Thess. 5:17). If a relationship with God cannot be sustained without communication, then a relationship between a parent and youth is not likely to be healthy without it.

Youth have a right to privacy. They are human beings, and most people require some privacy. Parents sometimes pry into every detail of every event of a youth's life thinking they are "communicating." Some parents feel that they must tell youth everything about themselves to be real and honest, but adults have privacy needs as well. Communication doesn't mean there never will be secret thoughts. It means that when the secret thoughts begin to influence the relationship, there will be enough trust and confidence for youth or parents to risk sharing them.

What Is Appropriate Discipline for Adolescents?

Love requires that parents discipline their children. The failure to discipline is both an unloving and ineffective way of parenting. Parents can discipline children in many ways. Some ways are effective for some purposes but ineffective for others. Some forms of discipline are effective at one age but not at another. The kind of discipline that is appropriate for youth depends on what kind of goals a parent has. The identification of goals is the first step in determining appropriate discipline.

Parenting Goals. Parents and youth leaders will do well to ask periodically, *What do I most want this youth to have as he or she leaves the influence of home and moves into the adult world?* Different parents and youth leaders, no doubt, will want different things. More than anything, some people may want their youth to conform to normal social expectations: go to college, marry a nice person, settle down, be active in church and community, avoid crime and divorce, rear children, get along in the world. Others may want youth to have a sense of purpose, mission, self-discipline, and inner direction. Some want children who become adults with aesthetic sensitivities, social graces, and hosting skills. Some adults want youth to be what they themselves most want to be: mechanic or professor, single or married, conformist or nonconformist. There are others who don't care about profession or marriage, but more than anything want their children to become adults of sincere Christian faith and moral character.

As I write these ideas, I'm thinking about my little girl, Jenny. She's very young now, but during the lifetime of this book, she will grow into youth. What do I want her to become? Is it fair or right of me to have convictions about what I want her to be? Or, are parental desires something I should keep out of my mind? The answer to those questions, for me, depends on the nature of parental desires. Some desires are wrong for me to maintain. I don't believe parents have the right to try to dictate occupational choice or marriage partners. Those are decisions a child will live with long after parents are gone, and parents should learn to be supportive rather than determinative.

There are some things, however, which I have a right to desire for Jenny, and I have the parental responsibility to engage in practices that move her toward them. I want her to be acquainted with the claims of the Christian faith. I want her to own those claims for herself, and let her life be conformed to them. I want her to have moral integrity, to be able to discern the true values of life, and to be able to live by them. I want her to be able to accept the creation God has made in her, and to take joy in it. I want her to know how to give love to others. Of course, I will love her no matter what kind of adult she becomes, but these qualities of life, faith, and morality are goals

I have in mind as I accept the responsibility of parenting her.

I'm comfortable with these goals because they are central to the gospel of Jesus Christ. When a parent wants a youth to grow toward the values to which Christ himself has called humankind, their parenting goals are valid. When parents make other priorities their parenting goals, problems emerge.

To have goals is not to dictate outcomes. Freedom, as has already been discussed, is a gift parents should give their children. That gift means parents cannot determine how their children will act as adults. Good parenting is never a guarantee that youth will become good adults. All human beings are given the right to choose evil and refuse the Water of Life. (See John 4:10.) Parents can use their influence to encourage youth in true-to-the-gospel directions. That is both a parental privilege and responsibility.

Discipline Approaches. Discipline is the way parents, teachers, and leaders of youth guide children and youth. Discipline can influence behavior, feelings, attitudes, and even ideas; it uses several tools, including punishment. Psychologists have categorized punishments into several kinds.

One group consists of strategies that are known as *power assertion*. This technique is defined as "physical punishment or any other exercise of physical or material power over the child (such as threatening loss of privileges and physically forcing the child to do or not to do something").[9] Power assertion techniques are appropriate for preschoolers and early elementary children.

A second type of punishment is *love withdrawal* which is "defined as nonphysical expression of anger or withdrawal of love (such as the parent's telling a child that she doesn't love him, or is angry with him, or her walking away in disgust").[10] Many parents use this strategy. When a child grows too big to spank, parents resort to love withdrawal. When a mother retreats to her bedroom after a verbal fight with her daughter and refuses any continued interaction, she is withdrawing love as a form of punishment.

Induction is the title frequently ascribed to a third kind of disciplining approach. It involves "pointing out to a transgressor the consequences of his behavior for other persons."[11] It includes explaining the "why" of a transgression: why a particular act or attitude is wrong; why it hurts other people; why it can be detrimental to the child. If you wonder whether or not this kind of lecturing is really a punishment, ask a youth! Most will testify that lectures do, indeed, qualify as punishments. A desirable variation of the induction method is to ask the kind of questions which result in youth giving themselves the lecture. (For example, a parent may ask, Why do you think I have required you to call if you're going to be late?)

Effects of the Three Approaches

Power assertion is an effective strategy for control. Spankings have an influence on young children, but I believe physical punishment is inappropriate for older children and youth. Power assertion techniques, such as withdrawing privileges (grounding) usually are effective deterents against undesirable behavior. Withdrawing privileges is an acceptable, and sometimes necessary, form of punishment.

The problem with power assertion is that when the parent's power is gone (a high school senior graduates and goes away to college or youth are out for an evening away from parents) the behaviors it controlled may quickly reappear. Power assertion teaches youth that behaving is something to be done when there is someone around who can exert power over them. If there is no one to punish them, they might be inclined to engage in the punishable behavior. It doesn't produce a sense of morality or ethics. Another problem with power assertion techniques is that, as youth get older, parents have less and less power to assert.

Unfortunately, the only discipline approach which some parents know is power assertion. As children grow to be older youth, these parents continue to discipline them the same way they did when they were preschoolers. Studies have indicated that power assertion may be effective for controlling behavior when the parent's power is obvious to a youth. It is counter-productive in helping youth to become self-disciplined, to have appropriate feelings of guilt when they transgress, or to develop a sense of morality.

Love withdrawal has been demonstrated to be an effective discipline technique. It is particularly powerful in developing a sense of guilt. The problem is that many youth who are punished by love withdrawal develop disproportionate feelings of guilt. These feelings, when combined with feelings of personal inadequacy can become so overwhelming that a youth can be afraid to exert him or herself or express any independence. While some guilt is necessary for healthy human functioning, guilt should not be the primary goal of parenting. Parents who use love withdrawal probably aren't aware that they are teaching their children to feel extremely guilty. They may use love withdrawal because their parents used it or because it seems more gentle than physical punishment. The constant use of love withdrawal can be a cruel form of punishment to a sensitive youth.

Love withdrawal also seems to be a strategy which Christian parents and leaders of youth must evaluate in terms of their faith. Christians never have God's love withdrawn from them—even when they fail. Christians are called to love all people, and are not excused from that calling. Christian parents will find it difficult to defend withdrawing their love from anyone, let alone their own children. Of course, love withdrawal does not mean that parents stop loving their children. It means that they withdraw from expressing it and from extending its benefits to their youth. It is difficult to find a biblical affirmation that Christian parents ever have the right to stop expressing their love.

Induction, the third disciplining strategy, is more frustrating for parents to use, but is more effective in accomplishing certain parental goals. The use of induction—helping youth evaluate why something is wrong—contributes to youth's acceptance of responsibility for wrongdoing, understanding of right and wrong apart from external rewards or punishments, willingness to confess, and appropriate levels of guilt over wrongdoing.[12]

Confessing wrongdoing, understanding right from wrong, and feeling appropriate guilt for wrongdoing are necessary if youth are to become persons of moral commitment. They are important qualities for understanding the offer of God's saving grace. Confession and repentance of sin are hardly possible without these characteristics. And salvation is hardly possible without the willingness to confess and repent.

While psychological research suggests that induction is an effective disciplining strategy, it is also difficult and awkward. Sometimes, it seems like the discussions do so little good. Behaviors don't change as quickly as parents wish. Research suggests that, *in the end*, induction may be the most effective of the three discipline strategies that have been discussed.

Focus on Christian Parenting

Long-term goals must be the constant focus of Christian parenting. They cannot be sacrificed for more efficient methods of short-term control. "Train up a child in the way he should go: and *when he is old*, he will not depart from it" (Prov. 22:6). Many parents don't really like that verse. They would rather have assurance that training

69

their children the right way will mean that they will never doubt faith and morals as high school seniors, or have a wayward young adulthood. The wisdom is that when the child "is old" the benefits of prudent childrearing become evident. One Old Testament scholar has noted that this verse is not a guarantee that a child will grow up acceptably. "A son may be too arrogant to learn (Prov. 13:1; 17:21); a wicked son may make fun of his parents (Prov. 30:17), run through their money (Prov. 28:24), despise his mother (Prov. 15:20), curse his father (Prov. 30:11), or turn his mother out-of-doors (Prov. 19:26)."[13] The verse is an admonition to train up the child, and to refrain from evaluating the effectiveness of that training until old age.

The teaching of Proverbs also identifies which forms of discipline are helpful. Proverbs 13:24, RSV, probably is the most quoted verse on discipline: "He who spares the rod hates his son; but he who loves him is diligent to discipline him." The verse should not be interpreted to mean that the only form of punishment is physical, nor that physical punishment is the form of discipline most advocated by Scripture. Proverbs also presents a clear picture of what the psychologists have called "induction":

> Hear, O sons, a father's instruction,
> and be attentive, that you may gain insight;
> for I give you good precepts:
>   do not forsake my teaching.
> When I was a son with my father, tender,
>   the only one in the sight of my mother,
> he taught me, and said to me,
> "Let your heart hold fast my words;
> keep my commandments, and live;
> do not forget, and do not turn away
> from the words of my mouth.
> Get wisdom; get insight.
>   Proverbs 4:1-6, RSV

Teaching is always more difficult than controlling. Instruction is more time consuming than physical punishment. Parenting should bequeath the gifts of insight, wisdom, responsibility, moral integrity, and openness to the Christian calling to youth. That bequest is made through the discipline of correcting, instructing, explaining, calling to accountability, and doing them over and over. Power assertion by the withdrawal of privileges may be necessary from time to time. It

is an appropriate strategy for adolescent children. Youth, however, have developed the ability to think logically and abstractly, and induction should accompany all discipline. If parents have no reason for forbidding a youth from an activity, then perhaps parents should reconsider their decision to forbid. If parents don't know why they said, "No," the appeal to parental authority (Don't do it because I said not to do it!) will not be very convincing to youth.

Family and Today's Youth

The joys and pains of family life comprise an arena where "today's youth" seem to differ very little from yesterday's youth. Southern Baptist youth have been describing their feelings toward families in a survey instrument since 1969. Those youth who completed the instrument in 1980 did not differ in their attitudes from those who completed it in 1977, 1974, and 1971. It does not matter how different youth of the 80's may be from youth of the 60's or 70's, their worries and joys about family life remain quite unchanged.

These consistent scores reflect the degree of concern which some youth express, high school generation after high school generation. About one third of these Southern Baptist youth said that they were bothered (either "very much" or "quite a bit") because they sense "a need for a greater feeling of love in their family." About 25 percent were bothered because they didn't "feel that their parents trust them."

Southern Baptist youth also expressed a consistent degree of contentment with family life. An overwhelming majority feel loved and trusted, and do not worry more, on the average, than other youth about family spats or relationships with parents. Home is a good place. Youth express contentment that family members are close to each other, mothers and fathers are interested in them, and the family gets along fairly well.

The picture is not unlike the discussion at the beginning of the chapter. After all the complaints, the majority of Southern Baptist youth feel that they get along with their parents. What more could parents ask for than that their youth say, "I've come to the realization in the past year or so that my parents try to be pretty good?"

Personal Learning Activities

Complete the following statement with words or phrases that define what stable family relationships give to youth.

Family is . . .

List the names of persons in your childhood including family and yourself. Beside each name, list the roles that person has, then the influence that person exerts on the family.

Family Members   Roles   Influence

How many of the youth with whom you work live with only one parent?

What influences are they missing?

How can you help provide for the needs of these youth?

Aleshire has listed three parental characteristics which contribute to positive growth for adolescents. List them and write an example of how each affects youth.

1.

2.

3.

List three approaches to discipline and the effects of each.

	Approach	Effect

1.

2.

3.

Which approach is used most by the parents of the youth you know?

Growing Up in American Schools

5

Growing Up in American Schools

A Discussion with Middle School Youth

LEADER: What do you think was the hardest thing that happened to you when you first went to middle school?

YOUTH: Meeting the teacher.

Youth: The hardest thing for me was . . . I had two people I knew in my whole school . . . and the hardest thing for me was . . . just getting up the guts to start talking to people.

YOUTH: For me, I had to get bused in the sixth grade. I would have gone to an elementary school in the sixth grade, but I had to get bused to a middle school and it was so hard because you went to a new school . . . it was downtown and it was sort of scary and everything.

YOUTH: Well, I mean some teachers, like they started out being really nice and then there was this one, I won't mention any names, who started out really super mean. . . . My

LEADER: really bad teacher that I really hate, she's starting slowly getting better.

LEADER: Let's hear from the eighth graders. What's happened to you as you stayed in middle school?

YOUTH: I love it. I went there and was really scared. I thought I wouldn't know anything. I felt smaller than anybody else. But when you are in the eighth grade, you're not. Nobody's a kid any more. You just walk around and do whatever you want to do. You just don't feel scared or anything, you know almost all the teachers in the whole school.

LEADER: Do you like to go to school more now in the eighth grade than you did in the sixth grade?

YOUTH: Yeah.

LEADER: What about the seventh graders. What's the best thing about being a seventh grader?

YOUTH: You can look down on the sixth graders!

A Discussion with High School Youth

LEADER: Apart from drugs, what do you think is the biggest problem youth are facing?

YOUTH: The school system. It's weak. Every time you turn around, they're threatening your graduating class. They say they are going to close the school. They're determined to break up your group. With budget cuts, busing and threats of closing, you don't really have enough time to develop a long-term relationship.

YOUTH: The teachers don't seem to be interested in teaching.

LEADER: Do you think you have more good teachers or bad ones?

(About two thirds of the youth said that they had more bad teachers than good ones.)

My discussions with youth in 1981 provided so many familiar memories: worries about parents and dates, battles between brothers and sisters, wondering about vocation and the future. When our discussion turned to the schools, however, the familiarity dissipated. All is not different, of course; but change has rampaged through American schools. If the youth I talked with are anything like American youth in general, going to school for "today's" youth really is different from what it was for yesterday's youth.

My personal school history was written during the days the post-World War II population boom was being educated. Schoolrooms were crowded. School districts were in competition with one another for teachers. Portable classrooms stood beside half of the brick schoolhouses in our community. My sixth-grade-year began with five weeks of substitute teachers while the district was trying to hire a regular teacher. Like the population, education was booming. Bond issues were passed with regularity. Buildings were built. Federal money was earmarked for education programs and the teaching of teachers.

It was an era when the American public appeared to have a great trust in education. They seemed to think it could solve both the world's and individual's problems. The American response to the Russian achievement of an orbiting satellite, for example, was a massive program of math and science education in American schools. Youth were encouraged to go to college as a way of securing their financial futures and a better life.

Of course, there were some hard times. The nation's painful awareness of the moral and personal effects of racial segregation were exceeded only by the pain associated with efforts to achieve integrated education. When all the grade-school children of the 1950's were in college in the turbulent 1960's, many people began to wonder about the value of higher education. In spite of serious problems, schools in the late forties, the fifties, and sixties were building, bustling, busy places.

It really is different in the early 1980's. Most school districts in the United States have declining enrollments. Closed schools are not uncommon sights in many communities. Across America each spring, the 6:00 PM local news covers the spectacle of parents and students protesting the closing of their school, and appealing a school board decision in the courts. About three miles from our house, there is a high school that closed at the end of the spring term. It is a large, twenty-year-old building which now stands empty. Some resentful youth painted a graffiti epitaph on the front wall in large white letters: FOR SALE.

Going to school brings some common experiences to American youth—even across different generations. School is an important aspect in adolescent life. It is a proving ground for a youth's sense of Christian discipleship, the arena in which some personal and social battles are encountered, and an environment in which success and failure are clearly marked. Some psychologists argue that school and family are the two most formative environments in a youth's world.

Youth and Schools

Growing up in American schools influences youth in many ways. The schools provide a wide assortment of youth from which friends and foes will emerge. Schools can give a youth an overwhelming sense of accomplishment or a degrading sense of failure. They give youth opportunity for serious competition with other youth. They introduce youth to adults outside the home who will likely influence them a great deal.

Schools provide the community where youth learn values from peers which they never learned at home; where youth sit beside people they would likely never live beside; where hopes, dreams, and fantasies never imagined at home become a frequent topic of discussion. These are the kinds of influences which do not change much over the years, and are important considerations for an understanding of youth.

Friends and Foes

Although they are not on the academic schedule, joys and pains of friends and foes absorb a great deal of an adolescent's school energy. Merton Strommen conducted a study of over 7,000 high school age church youth, including Southern Baptists. Several questions in that study asked youth to register their feelings of concern about relationships at school. He found that 53 percent were concerned that "Classmates at school could be more friendly." Fifty-one percent were concerned to some degree that "Some classmates are inconsiderate of my feelings." Fifty percent expressed some concern that "I feel pressure at school to do what others do."[1] About 28 percent of church youth are bothered because they "do not have many friends at school."[2] These feelings of concern appear to be relatively stable over the years.

Gaining recognition from friends, living in ways that will attract their attention, and exhibiting the characteristics they think are desirable are important issues for many youth. A 1979 nationwide study[3] identified the feelings of 3,308 seniors about how status was achieved in their high schools.

These data reflect some interesting attitudes on the part of youth.

The most important means to status for these high schoolers were: "Being a good athlete" (53.6 percent responded either "very great" or "great" importance). "Being a leader in student affairs (44 percent responded either "very great" or "great" importance). "Getting good grades" (43.8 percent responded either "very great" or "great" importance). The athletes, it would seem, have it made in American high schools. Imagine how difficult it may be for youth who want to feel accepted but have few athletic attributes! One intriguing pattern in these responses is that 43.8 percent said that getting good grades was important for high status, but only 22.3 percent said that knowing a lot about intellectual matters helps a student achieve status. Isn't that interesting? Getting good grades helps status more than knowing intellectual things. High schoolers apparently value grades more than they value knowledge or the ability to think!

School brings adolescents together. Usually, when adolescents get together, there are attempts to seek recognition, to conform and to live up to the expectations others have. A school influences youth by the peers who gather there each day.

Accomplishment and Failure

There are very few times in life when accomplishment and failure come with such clear signals as they do in school. For example, while many adults are evaluated in their jobs on a periodic basis, very few are evaluated every six to nine weeks. Yet, that is the frequency of evaluation most youth experience. Every month and a half, the work of 30 hours a week is assigned a grade in relation to some standard. *A's, B's, C's, D's, F's*—all are flags and symbols that brothers and sisters, parents and teachers, prospective employers, and college registrars will consider. Grades provide the opportunity for a great sense of accomplishment (I got four *A*'s this term!) or a terrible sense of failure (I got two D's and an F). The feelings of failure don't require *F*'s. Some youth and their parents construe any grade below an *A* or a *B* as failure. For such a youth, a report card consisting of three *B*'s, an *A* and a *C* can be devastating.

One reason grades and athletic ability may be as important to youth as they are is that they are so obvious. Everyone can watch a good athlete or look at someone's grade on a test. These criteria allow easy clarification of youth into groups. Some groups (like the varsity letter club) signal achievement. Other groups (the "no-names," as the youth in one discussion called them) signal failure.

Grades are *associated* with the attitudes youth maintain about themselves. Strommen found that church youth who "get low grades, who are unable to concentrate on their schoolwork, and who worry about their academic performance usually rank low in self-esteem."[4] He continued to speculate that low grades probably don't cause negative feelings of self-worth. They do, however, provide "proof" to students who do not feel good about themselves that they are of little worth. The power of both grades and athletic ability is in the importance others ascribe to them, and the ease with which youth can be categorized by them.

Competition

Competition is both admired and feared in American society. It is admired by many individuals who see it as the backbone of the American economic system. Competition makes for better products, better choices, better skills, and better people. Competition can be an incentive that spurs youth on to greater individual achievement. Other people have some fear about what competition does. They note that it can cause cheating and sin; it artificially makes some people into winners and others into losers, and even that it goes against the Christian principle of caring for one's brother and giving mutual support.[5]

Competition probably can be both destructive and redemptive. Whatever its effects, it is something abundant in most American schools. Debate teams and tryouts for the school play; first chair in the band or the solo part in chorus; the National Honor Society or the homecoming queen; basketball, football, baseball, or track; advanced programs or cheerleader tryouts—schools provide an abundance of competitive events which give some youth the occasion for victory and others the sting of defeat. Many youth (probably most) handle it all quite well. For some youth, however, loss is a crushing blow, and victory is an artificial elation. For all, the school environment teems with competition.

Other Adults

Many youth spend more time with the adults at school than they do with the adults in their families. School teachers and counselors are important influences in the lives of many youth. Some theorists argue that this influence is more pronounced for middle school/junior high school youth than for high school youth.

Donald McNassor has written: "Early adolescents will often remember with pleasure, or with deep resentment, some junior high teachers long after they have only misty memories of their high school teachers."[6] Teachers acquaint youth with a world beyond family. They become guides, and in some cases, friends. Youth will latch onto adults who take them seriously. This tendency is so strong that youth ministers, at times, have to work hard not to be pied pipers. Youth will gladly hear from some teachers what they refuse to hear from parents.

When the teachers don't take notice, the students do. Thirty-eight percent of church youth reported: "Some teachers are sarcastic and critical of what I do." Thirty-seven percent were concerned that "Some of my teachers do not understand me."[7] The acceptance and appreciation a teacher can give a youth is a powerfully positive experience. It helps youth feel good about themselves. By the same power, a teacher's failure to notice a youth or like her/him, can become a devastating hurt. Youth have a need to be accepted and appreciated. Teachers are the only adults who spend much time with some adolescents. McNassor concluded: "In the long distant past, children had such experiences with adults (contact with varying adults in varying roles) in the natural course of community life. Now, the school has to be the agent for planned experience with adults outside (the home)."[8]

Expectations of Schools and the Needs of Youth

Americans expect much from the public school system. They are frustrated and angry when the schools do not live up to those expectations. Some school systems are haughty and insensitive to parental concerns or student's values. Most schools, however, are comprised of caring persons who are trying to do what they think is educationally sound. Sometimes, parents and others in the community place unrealistic demands on the school system. Careful attention needs to be given to the expectations the public has of the school, and the needs of youth which the schools can meet.

Robert Havighurst and the committee on Human Development at the University of Chicago have studied the needs of youth over several decades, and identified possible educational responses to aid youth in completing their developmental tasks. The needs youth have, the responses schools can make, and the expectations the public maintain frequently seem to be in conflict. The following paragraphs identify four of the several developmental needs which Havighurst thinks the schools should address, and the controversies that emerge as schools deal with these tasks.

Sex Role. Males need to learn about masculinity and females about femininity. The schools can address this task by helping youth understand the sex role options in American society. Some Christians, however, believe Scripture teaches certain sex roles; others believe that Scripture teaches emancipation from definitive sex roles. The debate at church gets carried to school. The schools are put in the difficult position of either ignoring the basic developmental need of defining sex role options or teaching options which some people will consider offensive. As schools begin to help youth learn sex roles, the expectations of a value-mixed-up society make their task all but impossible.

Emotional Independence. This developmental task is "to become free from childish dependence on parents; to develop affection for parents without dependence upon them; to develop respect for older adults without dependence upon them."[9] While much of this task must occur in the home, schools can help by: providing a "study (of) the conflict of generations in literature;"[10] encouraging teachers to be helpful adults during the process of weaning away from parents; and providing opportunities for parents to understand the developmental task and approach it constructively. This area, like the others, is value-laden. Conflict between parents and youth is sometimes a value conflict. To help youth deal with the conflict, the schools need to help youth evaluate their values and those of their parents. Teachers cannot help youth with value conflicts without teaching values. The values any teacher might support (more than likely) will be satisfactory to one group of parents and offensive to another group.

Preparing for Marriage. Youth need "to develop a positive attitude toward family life"[11] and gain home management skills. Schools can teach home economics, but their teaching of attitudes about courtship, marriage, and family is riddled with values. Our society seems to have accepted views of family life (like cohabitation) which are contrary to scriptural teaching. As an instrument of a society where some individuals endorse patterns like cohabitation, should schools inform students about all socially acceptable patterns of marriage? Or should they ignore the society and teach only those acceptable to Christians? The schools are the *only* place where many American youth can get any help with the ideas about family and marriage. The schools can't just ignore this developmental task. The minute they address it, however, someone will disagree with

their teachings.

Acquiring Values. Every youth needs to develop a sense of identity (as discussed in chapter 3). Havighurst has argued *(along with Erik Erikson)* that a youth develops identity by forming values about self, society, and the world. The response of school can be to ignore this need of youth. Or, as Havighurst has recommended, [they] "can help students acquire a worthwhile combination of . . . values that will maintain the positive qualities of a highly productive economy and add the aesthetic and ethical values which bring more beauty and love into the lives of people; (and) to help students learn how to apply these values in their personal and civic lives."[12] Now, the core of controversy has really been opened. Most people in our society want youth to formulate a sense of values. The developmental psychologists suggest that forming values is necessary for healthy psychological growth. Disagreement over which values should be taught is rampant.

Youth frequently find themselves caught in the midst of teachers who are afraid to say what they believe, or are required by school resolution *not* to say what they believe. Youth need to discover their values, but must do so in a society where values differ widely and where many groups are active to make sure *their* values are the ones legalized and taught in American schools.

Problems at School

It is a mark of today's world that the school's responses to these adolescent developmental tasks can become a community battleground. Because constituents who fiercely disagree with one another expect the school system to pass on their particular points of view, the schools are frequently in a no-win position. These conflicting expectations of schools mark a uniqueness in the American educational system of the 80's.

Today's Youth and Today's Schools

Maybe there never was a time when American schools could uniformly address the developmental tasks of youth without protest from some part of the community. Maybe everything is the same, except today's battles are publicized more widely. Somehow, however, it seems the schools have become more ideological battlegrounds than learning arenas—especially over the last thirty years. There are some trends which cause today's schools to be a different influence on today's youth than yesterday's schools were on yesterday's youth.

Declining Enrollments. Enrollments in elementary, middle, and high schools have been declining, and will continue to decline during most of the 80's. Projections for 1980 to 1990 indicate that there will be an increase in the number of young children, but a continued decrease in the number of younger and older youth (between 5 and 15 percent fewer in 1990 than in 1980).[13] If the projections hold true (and they will because the number of ten-year-olds in 1990 depends entirely on the number of babies in 1980—a known fact), the decade of the 80's will continue to be a time of declining school enrollments. Declining enrollments have a variety of effects.

School Closings. The senior high youth in the dialogue that introduced this chapter revealed the concern over school closings. Declining enrollments mean that some schools must be closed. Closing schools affects communities in many ways. Athletics, school alumni activities, community events, and the traditions passed on from one student generation to another are all influenced. The most profound affect is on the students. It is hard to be a first-string ball player for two years on a high school team, then be transferred to another school for a senior year where someone plays the position better. It is hard to have formed a group of friends who are eventually sent to three different schools because their school closed.

Faculties. Declining enrollments also influence teachers. Many districts have a last-hired-first-fired policy. When a school is closed to save money, faculty positions are eliminated. The teachers with the longest service records are the ones who keep the remaining jobs. The result is an older faculty, many of whom are in the higher paying salary tracks due to years of service and merit increases. Faculty morale often is low because teachers worry, year after year, who will be laid off next. Teachers with these worries and frustrations can't spend hours a day with youth without their concerns becoming obvious to the youth. The result is that the youth are affected in subtle, undefined ways.

Budget Cuts. The public has a right to expect the cost of education to decrease as the enrollment does. The relationship is not as direct as it may seem. Two classes of thirty-five fifth graders may dwindle to two classes of twenty-five each. Good education would be difficult for a fifth-grade class of fifty. Even though the number of fifth graders decreased by one third, it still takes two teachers to teach them. Some consolidation can take place, but it seldom can be enough to make the teacher reductions in the same ratio as student reduction. Because many state legislatures fund public education on a per student basis, the money going to schools is reduced at the same rate the enrollment is reduced. The result is that budgets must be cut; that means programs must be cut.

In the school district where I live, the budget cuts are coming out of athletic, music, and art programs as well as school closings, teacher, and administrator layoffs. The effect on the youth I talked to was evident in some feelings of discouragement and a sense of having been cheated. "If I had been in the tenth grade five years ago, I could have gone to the festival in the eastern part of the state. We couldn't go this year because there wasn't any money." Of course, the youth are going to make it. The youth of the 30's made it through the Depression, the youth of the 40's made it through World War II, and the youth of the 80's will make it through the budget and program cuts.

Courts and the Schools. A familiar phenomenon in many American communities is legal action involving school systems. Since the 1954 Supreme Court decision that racially segregated schools were illegal, the schoolhouse has been in the courthouse. Desegregation suits, suits by teachers being fired or laid off, suits by interest groups wanting the schools to teach a particular theory or refrain from shelving a particular book in the library have been in court. Also, there have been suits to stop school closings, suits to keep prayer

87

out of schools and other suits to put prayer, Bible reading, and the Ten Commandments in the schools—American schools have a longer court record than most convicted felons! Legal action takes a toll on the youth. Many of today's youth will date their school days by the time their school closed, or when they protested a court order or school board decision.

Where is the red brick schoolhouse?

Multiethnic. Many American high schools are becoming increasingly multiethnic. The influence of Vietnamese, Laotian, and Cuban refugees, as well as the immigration of Puerto Ricans and Mexicans have influenced the overall constituency of Southern Baptists. Southern Baptists have started Korean, Vietnamese, and Laotian congregations, as well as Cuban Spanish, Puerto Rican Spanish, and Mexican Spanish congregations. In fact, in the United States, Southern Baptists worship in over seventy different languages. Evangelism has been most effective with people who have been able to learn and worship in their own language.

The eagerness to start non-English congregations has not been shared by the broader community with respect to the schools. Much debate has been made about whether schools should be bilingual or not. Many youth do go to school where English is not the only language spoken. Thousands of Southern Baptist youth speak Vietnamese, Korean, Laotian, Chinese, or Spanish at home and at church, but they must be able to learn in English at school. For Anglo-Southern Baptist youth, the presence of non-English speaking minorities creates mission opportunities for churches and associations, and conflict in their community school systems. Belonging to different ethnic groups can create powerful bonds and barriers.

Busing. Most of the youth I know will be bused at least two years of their public school career. Busing is a controversial topic in most communities. It is an attempt to insure equality for American society by meaningful integration in the schools. The goal is noble, but the method is hotly debated in most of the communities where it has been implemented.

The youth I talked with did not seem as bothered about busing as they were about other school issues. Youth have a capacity to adjust and make the best of things. But there are problems. Busing frequently extracts both Black and White youth from their community and the community-based activities that relate to schools. It influences the kind of friendship patterns that emerge. Distance keeps some youth who might be friends at school from continuing their friendship away from school.

Perhaps the biggest influence of busing in the lives of youth is the response of the adult population. Angry protests by adults teach youth a great deal, as do thoughtful reactions to governmental efforts to solve social problems.

Busing is one of the most confusing and complex issues in American society. Its disadvantages are obvious. Its advantages are subtle and long-term in the making. For many Southern Baptist youth, busing remains a part of their school day's reality.

Private Schools. Fifteen years ago, very few Southern Baptist youth attended private schools. The percentage who do is increasing. Three major reasons likely contribute to the increase. First, schools appear to many conservative Christians as secularized environments where Christian values are not taught. Second, many parents would rather have the tuition cost of private schools than to have children bused long distances. Third, the declining academic standards in some American public schools has led families to seek schools where academics are seriously enforced.

Many churches have started schools. Sometimes, good ministry reasons support their efforts. Other times, more negative motivations may have been at work. Whatever the case, some Southern Baptist youth now find themselves going to school and going to church at the same place. That changes the influence of both church and school.

Church used to be a place where youth were accepted as they were, encouraged to participate, appreciated for their presence, and kept accountable to only a few basic behavior standards. Rules, regulations, and performance expectations are required for good schools. There is an entirely different feel to a quality classroom where students pass and fail, and a Sunday School room where people are encouraged to accept Jesus as Savior. Church-related private schools impose a new set of standards for carrying out youth ministry.

When youth attend school in the same classrooms in which they have Sunday School and Church Training, they tend to tire of the environment. Teachers and leaders need to work extra hard to change the setting and provide a different atmosphere for church activities. Familiarity tends to breed contempt. The youth who attend the church school sometimes take on airs of spiritual superiority or indifference to church youth activities. Youth who attend other schools sometimes feel left out, not part of "the youth group." Sometimes, there is a general loss of respect for the house of God. The church is not special.

In most youth groups today, the youth are in several different schools, some private and some public. Building a sense of relatedness and wholeness in the youth group is not easy. Youth tend to assume some of the attitudes their parents have about public and private schools. Some parents have strong feelings about the values of public schools in preparing youth for life. Others feel private schools better prepare youth academically. Among some youth there is a desire to attend a private school their parents cannot afford. Thus, class or economic concerns divide the group. Leaders of church youth activities must be sensitive to the feelings of youth and their parents and seek to develop a cooperative accepting, and loving spirit among all the youth.

Conclusion

This chapter has captured my attention in several ways, as it may have captured the reader's attention. Much of the anger and frustration that existed in American society during the late 1970's and early 80's has found its focus in the American school system. In the last part of the twentieth century, American youth will be troubled with many problems in school.

School is an important and influential environment. The pluralism of an increasingly diverse society strikes a stunning blow in school-rooms and PTA meetings. Christian youth, and youth who need to be Christian, stand in the middle of it all, trying to grow up, trying to figure out what is the Christian thing to do.

Personal Learning Activities

How have schools changed from the time you were a youth?

What are some of the negative influencers of youth in the school environment today? How can church leaders counter these influencers? In the space provided, write the influences and how the church can counter them.

Negative School Influence   Positive Church Influence

1.

2.

3.

What are some positive influences of schools today? How can church leaders support and encourage these? Write them below.

Positive School Influences   Church Support

1.

2.

3.

What problems are encountered when youth go to church and school in the same place?

Growing Up with Friends and Enemie

6

Growing up with Friends and Enemies

From a Discussion with Middle School Youth

LEADER: What do you think is the biggest problem faced by most of the kids in your school?

YOUTH: Peer pressure, teachers, grades, other people. I know one guy who is really sensible, but he wanted to associate with a bunch of kids who are into punk rock and are really weird. He started doing that . . . I wouldn't be surprised if he was on drugs now.

LEADER: What are cliques like at your school?

YOUTH: There is one clique who are interested in studies, and another in social life.

YOUTH: There are two in my school. There's prep and there's punk. Punk doesn't mean you are going crazy; it's just that you are not a prep. Punk means you wear jeans and a shirt to school. You don't wear high stuff. Prep and Punk is what you are.

YOUTH: In our class, there's the type you don't like. You cut them down a lot.

From a Discussion with High School Youth

LEADER: What bothers you about people your own age?

YOUTH: They won't leave me alone and keep putting pressure on me.

LEADER: How many of you feel like you get pressured a lot from people your own age?
           (About half of the youth raised their hands.)
           What else bothers you about people your own age?

YOUTH: Sometimes, people can be dishonest, and hurt you.

LEADER: How many of you feel like you've been hurt pretty badly by someone your own age in the last five or six months?
           (About half of the youth raised their hands.)
           What else bothers you?

YOUTH: Sometimes, you get left out.

LEADER: What's your biggest fear?

YOUTH: Not being liked.

YOUTH: Getting stepped on.

YOUTH: Dying.

YOUTH: Boredom.

LEADER: How many of you figure you probably are in one kind of clique or another?
           (Most of the youth nodded or raised their hands to say yes.)

YOUTH: You're afraid to get out of your group to meet other people. Afraid of not being accepted.

Moving out of the security of a family into a world of peers is frightening, like just about every other change that comes with adolescence. Peers begin to exert pressure during adolescence, and that influence can continue for a lifetime. Keeping up with the Joneses is nothing more than an adult rendition of the adolescent peer group phenomenon.

Friends are an important part of youth's lives. They provide affirmation, security, and a sense of identity. Friends also can bring hurt, rejection, and isolation. Foes are important, too. Youth sometimes discover much about themselves by dealing with enemies. The experience of anger, vengeance, injustice, and gossip bring hard lessons.

95

Those lessons teach a great deal. Friends and foes and groups and cliques are part of the American adolescent experience. This chapter will explore their impact on youth.

The Function of the Peer Group

"Therefore a man leaves his father and his mother and cleaves to his wife, and they become one flesh" (Gen. 2:24, RSV). So, God ordered the generations of his human creation. People would leave families and start new families who would bring new people into the world, who would leave their families and start new ones. God ordained the family, but left it to human societies to fashion the ways in which the tasks could be accomplished. Twentieth-century American society generally has encouraged a gradual movement from the family of one's birth to the family of marriage and parenting. The adolescent peer group plays a variety of roles in the midst of the transition from childhood to adulthood.

Peer groups are not invented during adolescence. Preschoolers have playmates and elementary school children have friends. But the function of age-mate friends changes for adolescents. The peer group assumes an importance for both younger and older youth which it did not have during elementary school years. The peer group becomes a basis for authority, information, recreation, relationships, and identity. Each of these functions deserves some attention.

Authority

The authority a youth accords the peer group is, perhaps, the most disturbing aspect of the peer group for parents and leaders of youth. Most school-age children place total authority in parents and other adults. For example, if one third-grade boy tells another that the sky is gradually turning green, the other child will check out the observation with an adult authority. "Billy said the sky is turning green; is that true?" the child will ask a parent or teacher. The voice of authority—the person who settles the conflict—usually is that of an adult. By contrast, a tenth grader is likely to look to his or her peers as the authority—especially for advice concerning clothes, music, and appropriate behavior.

What many do not realize is that the authority of the peer group appears to be transitional and limited in its scope. Growing up emotionally is a process that starts with total dependence on parents

96

and moves toward a healthy independence from them. The peer group serves as an intermediate authority between youths' dependence on their parents and their own adult independence. By the late teens, the authority is not nearly as powerful as it was during early and middle adolescence.

Status

Peer group membership also identifies a youth with a particular status. In studies of youth peer groups, most youth can report the group they feel they belong to, and can rate the various groups in their school in terms of the prestige or status each has.

Some studies suggest that most American high schools have several status groupings out of which peer groups form. In most schools, the highest status is ascribed to the athlete or the brainy/athletic (the all-American ideal) group. High status also is ascribed to the social power group, which may be comprised of the attractive, more affluent youth, as well as the cheerleaders, beauty queens, and so on.[1] Roger Karsk, in a study of the youth in one Maryland community, found one peer grouping of the "smarts" (the youth who were brainy and participated in music, drama, choir, and other cultural events at school); another peer group comprised of drug users ("acidheads" or "users"); and others formed either on the basis of a pronounced philosophical position (the radical) or among youth who lived in a particular neighborhood. Karsk noted that minority youth, such as Blacks in a predominantly White school, or the very poor were also relegated to their own groups.[2]

Peer groups tend to be comprised of persons pretty much the same age and from similar economic backgrounds. Because peer groups form due to similarity of age, economic station, and so forth, youth frequently become part of a peer group on the basis of criteria over which they have little or no control. Some, because of father's income, are relegated to a high status peer group. Others, because of family background or race, find acceptance only in a low status peer group.

There is both a bit of unfairness and reality in such a peer group status system. Unfairness exists because people are categorized into groups, whether or not individuals want to be a part of that group. It is realistic, however, because adult society does the same kind of unfair categorization.

Recreation

Peer group membership provides recreational activities.[3] They frequently take the form of "hanging out," or "fooling around" or going to someone's house. These are the unplanned and unstructured events that can occur because youth are a part of a group. The recreation role is an important function of the peer group. Informal gathering can lead to problems, of course. Youth can do foolish or dangerous things in the inspiration of the moment. For the most part, however, the recreation is not dangerous. It involves going to the shopping center or a park or somebody's house, or goofing-off, or talking. It's the kind of recreation that parents frequently would

like to have defined more clearly, but a kind that usually is not detrimental to the youth.

Information

Peer groups function as effective teachers. The subjects sometimes are frivolous, sometimes worthwhile, and sometimes dangerous. Youth do learn from other youth. There are some areas of learning where youth depend on their peer group as the primary teaching authority such as what dress styles should be worn, what kind of music is best, and so on. The information function of the peer group is greatest where the group is perceived as having authoritative opinions. The group may be the primary source of education concerning sexual expressions and attitudes. That the peer group functions as teacher doesn't mean it necessarily communicates the right information. It can be a prime miseducator of youth, and sometimes is.

Identity

Another important role the peer group provides is helping youth discern their own identity. Individuals develop their sense of physical identity by looking in a mirror. The reflection defines their features and physique, and gives clues concerning attractiveness and homeliness. Belonging to a peer group provides something of the same function. Youth learn who they are, in part, by the peer group to which they belong. Some psychologists assert that the peer group can "(1) assist adolescents in resolving their conflicts within themselves and with others; (2) teach them respect for competence; (3) instruct them in how to act in social situations; and (4) [provide] a source of feedback to youths about their personality and behavior.[4]"

Youth discover who they are partly by discovering what they enjoy doing, what they can do efficiently, who likes and enjoys being with them, whom they feel comfortable around, and who seeks their company. The peer group provides a forum in which these discoveries are made.

Summary

The peer group, then, provides several functions in adolescents' lives. It becomes an authority to many youth. Through the range of issues over which this authority extends, the peer group is *overwhelmingly* authoritative in *some* areas of youthful lives. Membership in a peer group also provides a youth with a sense of status. Sometimes, it is an artifically high status; other times it is a painfully low status. Providing recreation and information are two other functions of the peer group. Through the mixture of all these roles, the peer group *helps a youth define his or her identity as a unique human being.*

The Influence of the Peer Group

The peer group influences youth by the way it provides—or fails to provide—the functions that have just been discussed. It influences in other ways as well. Chief among these is that the peer group places pressure on youth.

The pressure grows out of the authority youth ascribe to their peer group and the need they have to be accepted by others. The need to be accepted means there is a fear of being rejected. This fear leads to a willingness to conform to a group's expectations in exchange for continued acceptance by the group. The pressure can take negative turns at times. With most youth—especially the ones church leaders are likely to encounter—it doesn't happen often. There *is* pressure, however, that relates to youth's feelings of being acceptable and likable. Pressure can lead to negative behavior because the rewards of acceptance by a group frequently are greater than the rewards of being affirmed and accepted by adults.

That the peer group exerts pressure is news to no one. The kind and degree of pressure it exerts may be different than many assume. Adults frequently overestimate the power of the peer group. Research indicates that the peer group is authoritative and powerful in some areas, but not in all of them. Understanding youth requires an understanding of those areas where the peer group is influential, and those areas where other sources of authority are the primary influence.

Major Areas of Peer Group Influence

One reason adults assume that peer groups have an all-powerful influence on youth is that their influence is concentrated in such obvious areas. The authority of peers is greatest in areas such as music, leisuretime activity, and norms for dating. Authors Smith and Kleine have concluded that peers have influence on decisions "about the courses to be taken and clothes to wear."[5] Dorothy Rogers has argued that youth are more inclined toward the opinion of their peers "in areas in which social values are rapidly changing . . . (and) when immediate consequences are anticipated."[6]

The battles indicate that an adolescent is responding to an authority pressure outside the home. Most youth are not just listening to particular music because it is pleasing. They listen because their peers have taught them it sounds good. Frequently, parents try to persuade their adolescent children to learn to enjoy another kind of music—but find the task difficult, if not impossible. The difficulty testifies to the power of the peer group influence.

Peer authority is indirectly reflected in a study of the attitudes and opinions of seniors graduating in 1979. Illustration 1 shows how much they saw their attitudes as different from those of their parents. These older youth said that their ideas were least similar to their parents' concerning what to do with their leisuretime, how to spend money, and what things are OK when on a date.[7] While less than half of the youth said that their ideas were similar to their parents in these three areas, more than half reported that their ideas were similar to parents' opinions in three other areas.

ILLUSTRATION 1
How close are your ideas to your parents ideas?

	Percentage of youth who said their ideas were "very similar" or "similar" to their parents	Percentage of youth who said their ideas were "different" or "very different" from their parents' ideas
"How you spend your money"	39.2	47.0
"What you do in your leisuretime"	43.4	52.2
"What things are OK when you are on a date"	46.6	39.2

Peer groups do influence youth, and do so strongly enough to pull a majority of youth away from the ideas of their parents. This strong relationship toward peer opinion does not extend to all areas of life. There are several areas where the majority of youth report that their ideas are very similar to those of their parents. Elizabeth Douvan and Joseph Adelson claim that the adolescent "is free to be 'teen,' that is to live in the consumption fairyland and to follow whatever strange customs the collective adolescent genius can dream up and the media popularize"[8] primarily in areas where the ultimate values are not at stake.

Because the influence of the peer group is so strong in such visible areas as music, appropriate dating behavior, and so on, some people have argued that there is a peer group "subculture" that separates the generation of youth from the generation of adults. While there is a peer-influenced culture among American youth, it would be inaccurate to conclude that the only influential factor in youth's lives is

the opinions of their peers. While there is peer influence, there is also parental influence. While there is an adolescent subculture (or many), there is also a mainline adult culture that many youth move toward.

Positive Peer Influences

Under the right circumstances, peer group pressure can be beneficial. For example, a magazine article a few years ago reported a problem of youth violence and some solutions that had been attempted. In one eastern state, county school officials felt that the best way to deal with vandalism and violence in the schools was through enlisting the help of youth. Students volunteered to spend their free time patrolling troubled areas. Their instructions were to avoid direct confrontation with anyone, but to report questionable activities to appropriate school personnel. The response was good from the students, and the presence resulted in less vandalism. While the student patrollers were likely not part of the offending students' peer groups, the project showed that youth can influence other youth in positive ways.

Another use of positive peer influence is demonstrated in programs such as the Peer Counselor Training Program of the Palo Alto Unified School District in California. This program involves the selection and training of some youth to be friends and helpers to other youth in the schools. Studies have suggested that some youth are so isolated from the adult world (they have been called peer-oriented youth) that only peers can share witness and ministry with them.

Churches need to seize the natural affinity youth have to other youth in their programs of youth ministry. Training youth to share their faith and to make visitors and prospects feel welcome and a part of the youth group—are all positive uses of peer group influence.

Negative Peer Group Influences

Of course, there are a number of potentially negative influences. The peer group can easily become a clique—with highly developed standards for inclusion and exclusion. Youth are so desperate to be accepted into some cliques that they will do things they don't want to in order to win acceptance. If the youth remains excluded, feelings of worthlessness and self-doubt may emerge. The clique can also have negative influence on the youth who feel safely accepted into it. Membership in a closed group can create a false sense of worth. When graduation comes, and the older youth is separated from the group that gave him or her so much sense of worth, feelings of alienation and self-doubt can flourish.

Cliques also can become a part of the youth group at church. They can form among the youth who are most active, or who are special friends, or who have been at the church the longest time. Cliques are both psychologically damaging and a sinful violation of the commands of Christ. Leaders, though their influence may not be strong in relation to a well-defined clique, should do all they can to minimize their negative influences. This may be done by (1) sharing the teaching of Scripture; (2) structuring activities so that youth can't easily divide into their own groups; and (3) providing adult support and acceptance to youth who may be excluded by their peers.

Peers can have a negative influence when they pressure youth toward non-Christian behavior. When I asked youth why their peers started using drugs, one responded that youth "wanted to be accepted by their friends." Another said, "You've got friends that do it so you experiment with it." Even though youth may turn to adults to help them determine what is morally right or wrong, they may do what they know to be wrong because their friends have encouraged them or have made it a condition of their friendship.

Major Areas of Adult Influence

The influence of peers is well documented, probably overestimated, and frequently quite spectacular. The influence of adults is more subtle, less obvious, and probably underestimated. Douvan and Adelson conclude that "Almost universally, our data show, the adolescent expects to rely on his parents for help and advice on deeply involving personal problems."[9] Illustration 2 shows the relevance of that conclusion for 1979 high school seniors. The responses of the 3,000 seniors were striking! Eighty percent of youth said that their ideas were similar to their parents concerning what they (the youth) should do with their lives.

ILLUSTRATION 2
How close are your ideas to your parents ideas?[10]

	Percentage of youth who said their ideas were "very similar" or "similar" to their parents	Percentage of youth who said their ideas were "different" or "very different" from their parents' ideas.
What should you do with your life?	70.7%	20.8%
What values are important in life?	75.6%	20.4%

While adults may feel helpless at influencing youth opinions about hairstyles, dress styles, or music, there is considerable evidence that parents can influence the values and life choices youth must make. Youth will protest that "adults are *so* dumb." When crises, or heartbreaks, or decisions with long-term consequences come, however, many youth are anxious to seek the help of adults.

It is important that youth leaders and parents not yield to the temptation to stop being adults in order to relate better with youth. Youth seem to look to their peers for advice on some issues and to adults on others. Leaders of youth and parents need to maintain their "adult" identification so that youth know whom to approach when life needs, spiritual crises, or moral values need to be discussed. Adults need to recognize that there appears to be some areas where they are influential, and should try to be available to youth to deal with them when they ask for help.

Summary

The result of this entire investigation into the role of the peer group is the discovery of variety. Peers exert strong influence in some areas, but create less pressure in other areas. The pressure they exert can have positive outcomes as well as negative ones. Understanding youth means that peer groups cannot be relegated easily to one all-powerful or all-encompassing role in the youth's life. Like almost every other area of adolescent development, peers have different degrees of influence on youth. Some youth are readily influenced to act, think, or feel any way the peer group suggests. Other adolescents are very adult oriented and seem completely untouched by peer pressure. General tendencies of groups of youth should never be construed as true for every individual.

Positive or negative, influential or not, peers are an important part of growing up. Recent surveys suggest that most youth do have good friends. For example, almost 83 percent of youth in one study agreed with the statement: "I usually have a few friends around I can get together with." About one third did report some degree of hurt concerning friends when they agreed to the statement, "I often feel left out of things."[11] Most youth seem to find a group of peers in which they have partners for recreation, teachers for various kinds of information, colleagues for sharing and talking, and associates in a system of support.

Because peers are important, loneliness and estrangement can be devastating problems for youth. Because peers are important, the gift of friends and community can be recognized readily and appreciated. Because peers are not the only important people in a youth's world, it is crucial that caring adults be ready to exert their influence, share their testimonies, relate their values, and point toward long-term hopes, dreams, and values.

Personal Learning Activities

Ask your youth what the status groupings are in their schools. List them, then rank them in terms of popularity, with *1* being most popular.

Groups   Ranking

What are the benefits of the peer group to an individual youth?

1.

2.

3.

How can the peer group influence be channeled by church leaders toward positive results?

Growing Up and
Faith Formation

R.R. Hester

7

Growing Up and Faith Formation

From a Discussion with Younger Youth

LEADER: If you could tell one thing to people who work with youth at church, what would it be?

YOUTH: Shorter sermons!

YOUTH: Give us the right to be crazy sometimes.

YOUTH: Let us have fun throwing paper airplanes out the window, and climbing chairs.

YOUTH: Stop using such big words.

YOUTH: We could all get together and make up our own sermon.

LEADER: What's the best thing about your church?

YOUTH: The people. They're friendly.

YOUTH: Some of our priorities are in the wrong place.

LEADER: That's not a "best thing," but let's talk about it.

YOUTH: I don't know, it just seems that the biggest part of our budget is for the furnace. It's either cold or 98 degrees. It just bothers me sometimes.

LEADER: What do you think some of your priorities should be as a youth group?

YOUTH: We need to do more than go on ski trips and stuff.

From a Discussion with Older Youth

LEADER: What would make your youth group ideal?

YOUTH: Well, there would be a lot of things—like initiative. There are too many times people get upset because they don't believe the youth can accept an idea.

YOUTH: Whenever we talk about this stuff in our youth group, someone invariably gets to the point of how it used to be; and that it's not nearly as good as it used to be.

LEADER: If I were a new kid in town and I visited the Youth II Department this morning, what could I have expected?

YOUTH: Probably most of us would have walked up and said, "Hello." This is the first church youth group I have ever been in. Before I came, everybody said how great the youth group was—and I was expecting a lot. But you don't always get what you expect (obviously disappointed). It just kinda makes you feel like you don't want to go back. A lot (of the problem) was expectations, though. I mean, if you have high expectations, and you want the group to live up to them, then you set yourself up to be let down.

Authentic faith helps youth to understand that life is a gift of God and that tomorrow is hopeful. It enables them to know that evil is evil and that goodness can infiltrate every crevice of wretchedness. Caring adults can hope for nothing more noble than for youth to accept the gift that God gives by grace. It can save them from destructive feelings and forces as well as the pit of lostness.

If the Christian faith were not as precious or noble, it might not hurt adults so much when youth miss the point, refuse the grace, and discard the gospel. The gospel is full of peace and love, of meaning and purpose, of celebration and justice.

Youth seem to think it odd that God would use the folly of preaching to proclaim the good news. (See 1 Cor. 1:21.) They can easily convince themselves not to listen to the preacher. The words that could change their lives go whirling by, crowded out by other words scribbled in the empty space of the bulletin.

This chapter is about the religion of adolescence. It will be understood best by those adults who have hoped and prayed and probably cried for some youth who shrugged off grace like last year's fad. Understanding adolescent dealings with faith requires adults' reflection on their own sense of faith. Understanding youth and religion also requires persons to remember that youth do not readily separate the content of belief from either the people who believe, or the institutions believing people create. Youth can react to a bad church, or sinful people in a church, by dumping the beliefs—even when the beliefs had nothing to do with the sinful behavior. Understanding adolescent religion includes understanding that Christian faith is never a clear-cut issue. It is tied to their relations to church, family, school, self, and peers. It is influenced by the maturity or immaturity of their emotions, and by their ability to think in new and different ways.

Youth and the Christian Faith

Faith should be for youth what it should be for adults. There is not one Christianity for youth and another for adults. Youth may be at different developmental levels or struggling with parts of faith that have become comfortable for some adults. Youth are nonetheless being called by the same Lord, according to the same purpose, toward the same ends. The exploration of faith for youth begins with an exploration of what is required for all true belief.

The Nature of True Belief

"He who believes in him is not condemned; he who does not believe is condemned already" (John 3:18, RSV). "He who believes in the Son has eternal life" (John 3:36, RSV). "'Men, what must I do to be saved?' And they (Paul and Silas) said, 'Believe in the Lord Jesus, and you will be saved'" (Acts 16:30-31, RSV). Believing, according to Scripture, is the crucial beginning point of Christianity. For youth, for adults, for anyone—the gift of salvation is activated by the gift of belief.

What does it mean to believe? *The Oxford English Dictionary* identifies many usages of the word *belief.* Two are of interest for Christians who believe. One is "the mental action, condition, or habit of trusting or confiding in a person or a thing; trust, dependence, reliance, confidence, faith." The second is "mental acceptance of a proposition, statement, or fact, as true, on the ground of

112

authority or evidence; assent of the mind to a statement, or to the truth of a point beyond observation."

Consider those two definitions. Is the belief that leads to salvation a belief *in* Jesus Christ—trusting him as Savior and Lord? Or is it a belief *that* Jesus is the Son of God, was crucified, buried, and rose on the third day? It is important for the Christian both to believe *in* and to believe *that*. Scripture suggests that the belief which saves is the belief *in—trust, confidence, total reliance on—*God through Jesus Christ. Elsewhere, Scripture states that "even the demons believe" (Jas. 2:19, RSV). They believe that Jesus is the Son of God and resurrected Lord. They know what truth is. Demons have no repentance, no trust or confidence in, no reliance on Christ. While both kinds of believing are a part of Christian faith, the faith that saves is the belief that is trusting in Christ.

Youth need to learn how to put their trust in Christ and to rely on him. Whatever else leaders of youth may want, they should want youth to be willing to trust Christ. That is the beginning of faith. If youth know the Scriptures backward and forward, but do not trust Christ as Lord and Savior, salvation remains an unreceived gift.

Saving faith is a matter of the heart. If youth are to be people of faith, they must be people who can use their emotions for the purpose of faith. "Beloved, let us love one another; for love is of God, and he who loves is born of God and knows God. He who does not love does not know God; for God is love" (1 John 4:7-8, RSV). Love is both the reason for and the result of Christian experience. To want youth to be Christians is to want them to know what it is like to be loved by the God of the ages and to have an increasing capacity to be loving persons.

Saving faith leads to ideas or propositions which are held as true. After people learn to believe *in,* they begin to be able to believe *that.* Scripture gives clear guidelines regarding what ideas Christians must affirm as true. The Spirit of God moved John to write: "By this you know the Spirit of God: every spirit which confesses that Jesus Christ has come in the flesh is of God, and every spirit which does not confess Jesus is not of God" (1 John 4:2-3, RSV). Later in the same chapter, he wrote, "Whoever confesses that Jesus is the Son of God, God abides in him, and he in God" (v. 15). To want youth to be Christian is to want them to be able to affirm the proposition that Jesus Christ is real, is of God, is the Son of God.

The faith that is true to the Bible involves more than thinking and feeling. It acts! The author of James wrote, "Faith apart from works

is dead" (Jas. 2:26, RSV). That admonition builds on earlier words in the letter: "Religion that is pure and undefiled before God and the Father is this: to visit the orphans and widows in their affliction, and to keep oneself unstained from the world" (Jas. 1:27, RSV). To want youth to be Christian is to want them to learn how to live and exercise their faith.

Saving faith is no respecter of age. It always entails trusting, thinking, feeling, and doing. Fifteen or fifty years of life do not change the nature of the believing process. The gospel always reflects grace and demand, love and judgment, hope and burden. Age does influence how individuals trust, think, feel, and act. Youth do not have the emotional maturity that adults do, so the feeling aspect of faith will be different with them than it is for adults. Youth do not think the way children do, so the thinking part of faith should change from childhood to youth.

This section explores each of the dimensions of faith—trusting, thinking, feeling and doing—with reference to the way youth experience them.

Trusting

Saving faith involves trusting Christ as Savior. Part of becoming and being a Christian is the ability to trust. Theologian William Hendricks has written, "Conversion is entering into a redemptive relationship with God through Jesus Christ. All redemptive relationships require trust."[1] "He that cometh to God must believe that he is, and that he is a rewarder of them that diligently seek him" (Heb. 11:6). To believe that God is and that God is a rewarder is to exercise trust.

Trusting Is Difficult for Some. Have you ever noticed that some youth have difficulty trusting? When youth have been surrounded by people who refused to keep their word or institutions which forsook their promises, they either do not or cannot trust anyone or anything. Suspicion, doubt, and cynicism flavor their approaches to life. People who find it impossible to trust can have difficulty trusting Jesus Christ as Savior. They may want to believe. They may want to accept Christ, but for some reason they just can't. Life has given them so many disappointments and broken promises. There is no energy left to risk one more promise—even though God is reaching out in grace to make it.

Occasionally, leaders discover a youth who trusts no one. These

115

youth may desperately want faith, but seem unable to reach out and trust God. Psychologist Erik Erikson has said that the first psychological crisis infants experience is a crisis of trust. They need to experience their infant worlds and bodies as trustable: food will come when hunger pains get strong enough; comfort and cuddling will come; their bodies will function. "Trust, then, becomes the capacity for *faith*."[2]

One of the characteristic reactions of early adolescents to their physical changes is a lowering of self-esteem. They don't feel good about who they are and find it difficult to trust themselves. Because they don't like themselves, many youth don't think anyone else could like them. For these youth, trust comes harder in adolescence than it did in childhood. Gordon Allport has observed, "Usually it is not until the stress of puberty that serious reverses occur in the evolution of the religious sentiment."[3] A variety of causes contribute to these "reverses" in religious faith, but the problems of trust for some adolescents may well be one of those reasons.

Helping Youth with Trust. Youth leaders can help youth with their sense of trust by being trustworthy and keeping their word and promises to youth. Leaders can discover what they can affirm and appreciate in youth, and continually remind them of those qualities. Steadfastly, leaders can care for youth—even when they do dumb things, show off, disrupt meetings, and cause trouble. Caring does not mean that leaders will never correct or chide youth. It does mean they will never reject them or withdraw love from them. As they experience the leaders' love, doubting youth may be more willing to risk accepting the love and care of God.

Leaders can't make youth trusting people, but they can avoid giving youth additional reasons not to trust. Leaders can be patient with youth whose faith, at its best, is like the father of the convulsing child, "Lord, I believe; help thou mine unbelief" (Mark 9:24). In an interview, Dr. Gisela Konopka said: "Trust is built slowly, through experience. When you are working with people, be honest. By that I don't mean be brutal. But be open; don't pretend the world is all good when you know it is not. When they need you, be available. It takes time to build trust."[4]

Thinking

There is considerable evidence that the kind of thinking individuals do changes during adolescence. (These changes have already been described in chapter 2.) Understanding youth and the Christian faith requires particular attention to these changes.

Changing Thought Influences Belief. Sometime during adolescence most people develop the ability to think in abstractions and to use formal logic. Of course, youth don't go around broadcasting that they have acquired this new ability. Some are better at thinking than others. Youth do acquire a new kind of ability, and it can revolutionize their understanding of the Christian faith.

More sophisticated ways of thinking make some want to throw away the concepts of faith they learned as a child. They had a childish idea of God as policeman or grandfather that their more mature way of thinking rejects. "If God is a great policeman or a push-over grandfather, then he's not much of a God," they conclude. So they decide God doesn't exist; or if he does, he is not what they learned about in Sunday School. Paul's admonition is appropriate for the youth's religious thinking: "When I was a child, I spoke like a child, I thought like a child, I reasoned like a child; when I became a man, I gave up childish ways" (1 Cor. 13:11, RSV).

Helping Youth Rethink Faith. Youth must be helped to avoid throwing away faith because their thoughts about it were childish. Children were created by the Father to have childish thoughts. They also were created to exchange their childish thoughts for more mature ones as they become capable of more complex ways of thinking.

God the grandfather must be replaced by a sense of God the Holy One, the Mighty One, the Loving One, the Just One. Prayers for bicycles and skates must be replaced by requests for God's will to "be done on earth as it is in heaven" (Matt. 6:10, RSV). For the first time, youth can begin to apprehend the church "as a fellowship of believers."[5] For the first time, youth can begin to understand grace, love, peace, justice, righteousness, providence, and sin. While there will never be complete understandings of them, the youth years bring the ability to understand more of them than childhood ever allowed.

Youth must translate the faith understanding they brought from childhood into new understandings that will carry them toward mature religion. For example, many early adolescents know most of the facts about Gideon and his army or about David and his slingshot. Those biblical events, however, are not just stories full of facts. They are the accounts of people struggling with faith and struggling with their relationship with a loving God. Gideon was trying to understand God's leadership, and muster up the trust to follow it. David was learning about belief in the God who gives victory and brings an end to the battles. Although the facts and details are minor parts of the lesson, they are the only part that children can learn. The lessons of trust, faith, following, victory, and vision must wait until the youth years, when logical thinking ability enables them to see the old story in new terms.

Unfortunately many youth assume that because they know the facts, they know the meaning of faith. When the Sunday School lesson is about David and Goliath, Moses, or Gideon, youth say, "Oh no, not again. We already know this. We studied about it as kids. Can't we do something besides this third-grade stuff?" The problem is that the youth know some facts and details, but they do not know their meanings. Their childhood minds—exquisite as they were—never allowed them to see the relationships, catch the majesty, or trace the subtle message of the lesson.

Youth ministry involves helping youth to use their more mature thinking ability to examine faith again. The youth will not be aware that their thinking has changed. A leader can't say, "OK, kids, use your new way of thinking to examine the text." A more subtle, patient leadership is required. Youth need to be guided, nudged, and encouraged to see beyond the surface facts. Leaders need to be painfully patient and understanding. Helping youth use their new way of thinking also means that leaders will need to use *their* thinking ability. Leaders need to be aware of the logic and integrity of their own religious thinking.

Feeling

Faith is trusting, thinking, and *feeling*. Christians are commanded to love God, to love neighbors, and to love themselves. (See Matt. 22:34-40.) Love is an emotional expression of humankind, and is central to the Christian faith. An important development in the faith of adolescents is the healthy maturing of emotions.

Faith and Youthful Emotions. Youth, as was discussed in chapter 2, are emotional creatures! Sometimes, they seem to be too emotional. Their emotions are not only extreme at times, but also they are unpredictable. Much of parenting and leading youth is to help them stabilize their emotions and to be more in control of them than controlled by them. This is true in their religious life as well.

Youth need to learn how to love themselves because changing bodies, unstable relationships with friends, and the pressure of school sometimes make it easy for them not to. Youth need to learn to love others in appropriate ways. "Appropriate" means that they learn not to sacrifice who they are morally, spiritually, or psychologically because they "love" a boyfriend or girl friend. Appropriate means that they learn how to care in unselfish ways, not in ways that get them what they want from others. Appropriate means that they neither underinvest nor overinvest in other people. Appropriate means that they learn to love in responsible and mutually constructive ways. Youth need to learn to love God. That involves obedience, commitment, discipline, celebration, and growing awareness.

When we take seriously Jesus' summary of the law in Matthew 22, the development of all three loves (self, others, God) is a part of youth's *religious* development. The nurturing of youthful emotions is crucial to maturing Christian faith.

Strangely, parents and other adults, who spend a great deal of energy helping youth stabilize their moods and feelings in other aspects of their lives, condone exaggerated emotions to bring about life-changing religious commitments. I am convinced there is no faith without emotion, but there can be emotion without true faith. Sometimes youth mistake emotional highs in a church setting as evidence that they are being faithful. There should be strong feelings in faith, but emotional highs are never adequate assurances that faith is alive and growing.

Helping Youth Feel Their Faith. When I was camp pastor one year, the camp director suggested that the youth talent show be scheduled to follow the main decision service. He had discovered that the emotions sometimes associated with a decision service influenced more than youth's relationship with God. They also felt close to each other, sometimes too close. Emotions are a part of humanity. There are no special emotions which ascend to God, just human ones which can be given to God or anyone else. Intense emotions can turn quickly from a God-ward direction to an earthly one. The talent show helped youth to use the emotions of commitment to God for sharing in mutual community celebration.

Youth need to use their emotions in their faith, but those emotions need to be tutored and directed toward a healthy, even keel. While generating intense emotional experiences for youth may seem religious, it can contribute to youth's rejection of faith later in life. A college student, for example, may conclude that his or her decision to be a Christian or missionary was just the result of an emotion; therefore, it holds no binding power as he or she enters adulthood. Commitments that are lasting—whether in marriage, with friends, or

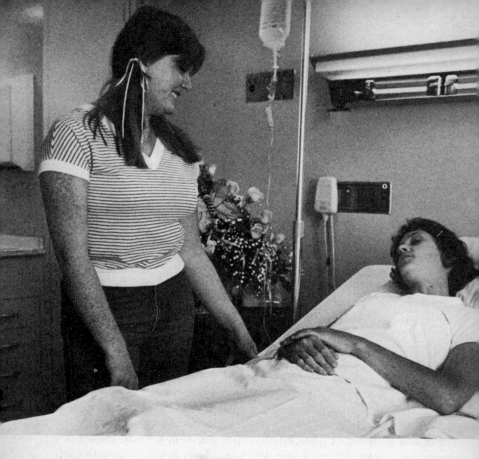

to God—require emotion, but they can never be merely emotional. Ministering to youth requires helping them develop appropriate and healthy emotions of faith.

Doing

Youth, if they are to grow to the biblical concept of maturity, "unto the measure of the stature of the fulness of Christ" (Eph. 4:13), must learn to live by their faith. Youth will not develop a mature faith by thinking, trusting, and feeling alone. They also must live their faith. John Westerhoff has said, "For faith, it is therefore especially important to acknowledge that the most significant and fundamental form of learning is experience."[6] He even argued, as a number of psychologists do, that behavior frequently influences thinking more than thinking influences behavior! Adults, for example, who have learned to tithe don't struggle to believe in its value. The behavior of tithing is the best way to learn the Christian doctrine of stewardship.

Youth need to be guided in living their faith. They need to be given opportunities to serve and minister. Sometimes, the best way to teach youth the gospel is to ask them occasionally to help teach it to the preschoolers or elementary school children. Sometimes, the only way to help youth learn about missions is for them to go on mission. Being part of Backyard Bible Clubs, Vacation Bible Schools, Big A Clubs, mission trips, choir trips, mission action projects, work projects, helping in Sunday School, helping in preschool and children's music activities, being study leaders or enlistment leaders in Church Training, or leading worship are effective ways for youth to learn and experience their faith. Some churches are tempted to provide a program for the youth that centers on teaching, fun, fellowship, and worship. Youth need all these, but they also need to express their faith and not always be on the receiving end.

Sara Little, along with other youth educators, has argued that youth need to participate both in service to a church and in the vision of the church to its community and world. "Youth who are members of the church are called to Christian discipleship *now,* as people of God placed in the world for ministry; they are a part of the ministering Body of Christ, within which they are supported and equipped for the fulfilling of their common calling."[7]

Conversion, Rededication, and Calling to Church Vocations

The call of Christianity—as Southern Baptist youth experience it at camps and revivals, youth retreats, Sunday School, Church Training, missions organizations, and music experiences—is a call to know Christ as Savior, to live holy lives acceptable to God, and to listen for God's possible summons to church vocations.

If youth have made a profession of faith as a child, that experience frequently is called into question during adolescence. If they have never professed faith, they will be encouraged to do so during youth years. Whether or not they are Christians, youth will experience new dimensions of sin. Many of them will seek to renew or recommit their lives as an act of repentance. While only a few are called by God to minister through church vocations, most youth will be admonished to listen carefully to determine if God is calling them to church vocations. These three expressions of religious experience—

121

conversion, rededication, vocational commitment—constitute the events in which faith takes on form and substance for many Southern Baptist youth.

Conversion

"Regeneration, or the new birth, is a work of God's grace whereby believers become new creatures in Christ Jesus. It is a change of heart wrought by the Holy Spirit through conviction of sin, to which the sinner responds in repentance toward God and faith in the Lord Jesus Christ." Those words are from *The Baptist Faith and Message,* and they clearly explain the outcome of conversion. Conversion involves a work of grace, a change of heart, repentance, and trust.

For many individuals, the adolescent years are really the first ones in which they become capable of conversion. If during childhood they were not aware of the evil of their sin or did not see a need to change, they could not be "converted." Awareness grows out of the convicting work of God's Spirit. Some children experience authentic awareness of their sin coupled with a desire to repent, but others do not. Adolescence, however, brings enough maturity and self-awareness that most youth can experience remorse for wrongdoing and a desire to deal with it.

Conversion is a special issue for Southern Baptist youth. Other theological understandings of God's redemptive work do not require a conversion experience. Baptist theology, however, as described by William Hendricks, assumes "an awareness of alienation from God, a recognition of God's provision for our salvation in Jesus Christ, and the cooperation of the human will with the divine will in effecting a conversion."[8] Many youth have problems with their faith because they "made a decision" as a school-age child, but did not see it at that time as a conversion experience. As their adolescent ability to think gives them more understanding about the nature of conversion, they begin to wonder if they are truly saved.

Sometimes, youth who wonder about their salvation are experiencing conviction for the first time. They may have made a decision as a young child in Bible School or during a revival, but that decision had its motivation in the responses of their friends or the pressures of the moment. It was not because they experienced the burden of their sin and turned to God for a change of heart and life. Whatever their decision, it was not a conversion as Baptist theology defines it.

Other times, youth who wonder about their salvation may have had an authentic experience of repentance and turning to God. Childhood sins, however, are not like adolescent sins. For example, the emergence of sexual desires introduces a whole new area in which sin can blossom. Family battles intensify during the youth years, and many youth who love both God and family feel guilty and burdened over their "new" sins of anger and hateful feelings. Some misinterpret this guilt as conviction, and assume that conviction only occurs when persons are in need of conversion. Such youth need to be guided in understanding that conviction comes freshly to the life of the sincere believer as sins emerge or reemerge. It does not mean the gift of grace has not been received.

Still other youth have an altogether different reason for questioning their conversion experience. They have experienced growth in their faith, and have come to a dramatically new way of understanding the Christian experience. The youth think to themselves, *If what I am now as a Christian really is what Christianity is about, then I must have never been a Christian!* Their conclusion is not appropriate, however. Biblical images abound with the idea that Christian faith matures, blossoms, and takes on new meanings as believers take it seriously. New levels of understanding or obedience do not weaken earlier levels of understanding.

A faith relationship with God has a certain similarity to a marriage relationship. A husband and wife who are committed to each other will experience altogether new levels of love and appreciation for each other as time passes. Those new levels of love and care do not mean they did not love each other when they decided to marry. A maturing faith relationship should bring new kinds of faith and understanding. Youth need to understand that they likely will experience new dimensions in their faith. That does not mean that the older dimension, although it certainly may have been less mature and correct, was totally wrong.

Youth frequently struggle with conversion. It is a fundamental religious issue. Sometimes, youth have never professed faith or experienced authentic conversion. Youth ministry to those youth includes a faithful, loving witness. Sometimes, youth have made meaningful professions of faith, but new sins or new understandings call that decision into question. Youth ministry to those youth requires the caring affirmation of the validity of their Christian experience. Such youth need encouragement to be open to the changes that have come as well as to those that are likely to come in the future. Leaders of youth need to be careful not to induce a kind of

"salvation anxiety" in youth. While youth need to explore the authenticity of their faith, they don't need to be constantly besieged with advice that raises doubt and suspicion.

Rededication
This religious experience is something which a large number of Southern Baptist youth encounter. Generally, it can be a positive way in which youth register a renewed obedience to the gospel. It also can be a way that youth acknowledge the presence of more

adult-like sins in their lives and confess them to the forgiving God.
Rededication may be a needed religious experience in a tradition that
holds to conversion theology, but also encourages young children to
make professions of faith. Baptists make much of the individual's
experience in relationship with God. Rededication is a way Baptist
youth redefine and reorient their experience of relationship.

Expressions of rededication also can be the result of manipulative
leadership by adults, an inappropriate theological understanding of
the walk of faith, or a means of getting attention by a lonely youth

hoping for acceptance in a church. Like youth's questions about conversion, questions and desires for rededication need supportive nurture and exploration by caring adults.

Youth need to know that the life of faith calls for many responses, not just the ones made during the invitation time in Baptist services of worship. Those are important times for important decisions, but they can be overused. Youth who make frequent rededications likely could benefit by counsel and help in exploring their sense of guilt, conviction, or calling.

Vocational Commitment

Adolescence is a time when many individuals first sense God's call to church vocations. That is the experience in my own life. When youth sense God's call, leaders can make several caring responses.

The first response is to help the youth "test" the sense of calling. Is it God's call or is it the youth's desire to live a "completely" obedient life? Some youth get the idea that if they really want to live dedicated lives, they will become pastors, missionaries, or ministers of education, youth, or music. Youth need to understand that God calls all people to the vocation of the Christian life (Eph. 4:1-6,11-13). Such a vocation demands radical obedience and constant commitment from all. People can be "completely" obedient and not be vocational ministers or missionaries.

If youth sense their call as a call to a church ministry, a second help leaders can provide is to introduce youth to the variety of expressions of ministry. Youth sometimes feel God has called them to be a pastor because that is the only church occupation they have observed. There are other expressions of vocational church service: ministers of education, music, Youth, Children, or Adults; missionaries, campus ministers, church program specialists, and so forth. It may be good to encourage youth to keep an open mind about the particular vocational ministry their calling may take.

A third aid adults can provide is helping youth identify their maturing gifts. Gifts and abilities will help youth define the direction of God's call. Youth need to be aware of their gifts and given the opportunity to exercise them.

An important gift leaders can give youth is encouragement: the encouragement to be patient and to be sure of God's leadership; the encouragement that youth *can* experience the authentic call of God; and the encouragement that God gives gifts that enable the call to be expressed.

Conclusion

In the experiences of conversion, rededication and vocational calling, the ministry of the leader of youth is to help youth think through the experience, to interpret it in light of Baptist expressions of faith and the witness of Scripture, and to provide a listening ear and supportive understanding.

Helping Youth Become Christian Believers

Nothing, no matter how much a parent or youth leader wants it, will insure that youth will mature to be faithful Christian people. God intended it that way. From the time of the Garden of Eden (Gen. 1 to 3:24), the Creator has given his human creation a choice. Youth are free to choose, to believe or not to believe, but parents and leaders of youth can encourage youth to accept the Christian faith as their own. Several factors have influenced adolescent religious development.

One study of high school youth from three denominations found that Southern Baptist youth reflected the most church commitment.[10] The authors concluded that Baptists consistently were stronger than the other denominations on several variables which were associated with religious commitment of youth. First, Baptist parents reported higher levels of participation than parents in other denominations. Second, Baptist youth reported that their parents talked with them more about church and faith than youth from other denominations reported. Third, Baptist youth reported liking past religious training more than others did. Fourth, Baptist youth perceived their leaders to be more sincere than youth in the other two denominations perceived their leaders to be. Fifth, Baptist youth held more clearly to their beliefs than other youth did.

Youth were asked in another study to identify the leaders of youth they most appreciated. These leaders were then surveyed regarding their motives, their methods, and the reasons for their effectiveness. Over half of them reported that their motives were religious: "I want to share my faith." "I can guide them to full Christian commitment."[11] Their methods included building relationships, being genuine, being available, showing interest, communicating with youth, and leading youth. These leaders of youth spent time teaching, creating a sense of community, and encouraging youth involvement as ways of providing youth ministry.

Merton Strommen thinks that three things are important in the process of helping youth in their lives of faith. One is to be a listener and guide as youth ask searching questions about faith. Leaders need to give youth the opportunity to use their newly developed intellectual abilities to rethink their faith, and anchor it in more mature ways of thinking. Another way is to provide items for reflection and decision. Youth should not be forced into commitments, but they should have an opportunity to contemplate their faith and the encouragement to make decisions regarding it. A third important factor is a congregation that takes youth seriously and provides a supportive ministry.

Following are some important things you as a leader of youth can do to help youth discover faith and grow in it.

● Be people of faith, and willing to share the meaning of faith, in your life. Think, feel, and act on faith.

● Be available, willing to listen as youth talk through feelings and emotions, even when the words are difficult and slow in coming.

● Guide youth in interpreting the proper place of emotion in faith—helping them to avoid the problems of too much or too little emotion.

● Do not try to be a youth, but allow youth to be youth.

● Involve youth in ministry and mission.

● Be patient. Youth is a time when many things come unglued. Youth need help gluing things back.

● Be affirming. Encourage the youth, help them see their gifts, remind them they are people who have been blessed and can be givers of blessings to others.

● Encourage parents not to leave religion alone at home. Nurturing faith cannot be something that happens only at the church building.

● Be Christian. The best way to tell youth about love, hope, and faith is to be loving, hopeful, and faithful.

● Be real, sincere, open, and trustable.

All of these behaviors do not guarantee that youth will be Christians. Christians, however, learn the story from others who know it and live it. For the last 2,000 years, that has been the process God has sanctioned for the proclamation of his love. Today's youth need the same gospel. The way God showed his love toward us—reaching to us while we were still sinners, loving us, sending his only-one-of-a-kind Son to incarnate that love—is the way faith can be shared with youth. Be gospel people.

Personal Learning Activities

Explain what it means to believe *in* and to believe *that* regarding faith in Christ.

What characteristics of youth enable faith and growth?

What are some elements of faith development which youth experience?

Look over the list of things leaders can do to help youth grow in their faith. Which of the items listed are strengths of your ministry with youth?

In what area are you weak?

How will you seek to improve?

Growing Up with Morals and Conflicts

8

Growing Up with Morals and Conflicts

A Discussion with Younger Youth

YOUTH: There's a lot of stealing in our school. I had my watch stolen out of my locker. I've had high school kids . . . come down the halls, and they come in and walk up to your locker and get something out.

LEADER: How many of you have a lot of problems with stealing in your school?

YOUTH: A lot.

LEADER: Everybody has? (*Most youth agree that just about everybody has.*)

LEADER: What do they take when they break in?

YOUTH: Lunch, jewelry, watches, homework.

LEADER: What do you think the biggest problem in the world is right now?

YOUTH: Ronald Reagan, Iran, war, nuclear weapons, poverty, hunger, fighting about abortion.

132

YOUTH: I'm not for abortion, but I'm not against it either. I think it's up to your own self.

YOUTH: This country's biggest problem is ERA. I'm for women getting equal rights, but who needs women getting drafted into the armed forces?

YOUTH: I'm for gun control.

YOUTH: But what do you do if you're walking downtown in a back alley and a man comes out with a knife at you? What do you do? If you whip a gun out at him, he'll take off.

LEADER: What do you think are the biggest problems you and other kids are facing right now?

YOUTH: Drugs.

LEADER: How many of you, if you wanted to get drugs, could get them from someone you know at school?

YOUTH: I don't know their names, but I know their faces. (*Most youth said that they would know who to talk to.*)

LEADER: What drugs are kids using?

YOUTH: Marijuana, speed, cocaine.

LEADER: What about alcohol?

YOUTH: Oh yeah, everybody does that.

A Discussion with Older Youth

LEADER: What do you think are the major problems with which the kids at your school are dealing?

YOUTH: Drugs, alcohol, school.

LEADER: How many of you would know who to talk with to get drugs?

YOUTH: I could get it Friday night.

LEADER: How many kids in your school do you think use pot?

YOUTH: Over half.

YOUTH: About 80 percent.

LEADER: What else do you really think troubles kids?

YOUTH: Sex. The girls come to school in these little skimpy things. (*everyone laughed*)

LEADER: Do you think high schoolers are really more sexually experienced now than they were twenty years ago?

YOUTH: Yes.

LEADER: What percentage of students at your high school do you think would have sexual union as a typical way of relating with a boyfriend or girl friend?

133

YOUTH: About 90 percent.
LEADER: Do youth have problems because of their sexual activity?
YOUTH: A lot of times girls think they are pregnant, and that causes a lot of problems.

The question came to young Joseph, who was engaged to young Mary, who found herself pregnant. *What is the right thing to do?* He wondered to himself. The angel of the Lord assured Joseph of the Miracle that Mary bore, and Joseph took Mary as his wife (Matt. 1:18-25).

Adolescence is a time when many youth struggle with the question that troubled Joseph. What is the right thing to do?

The questions are not just general in nature. They become painfully concrete at times. What physical affection is right to share, and what forms of affection are wrong? What makes some forms wrong? What substances are wrong to take into the body? Why would it be wrong to use them?

Youth also begin to ask serious moral questions about their nation and world. What should be done about poor people in the United States? What responsibility do Americans have for the poor and hungry people on the other side of the world? How should the problems of racism be addressed? What moral issues arise out of the expanding presence of nuclear weapons in the world, or the world's weapons bills?

While these questions may come with varying intensity to different youth, they do come to most youth at some time or another. Erik Erikson has said, "When you reach a certain age you can and must learn to be faithful to some ideological view."[1] While some people would disagree that there is a psychological need for moral values, few would deny the universal presence of moral standards in every human culture. Adolescence is the time when many youth embark on an exploration of moral options and determine which ones they will affirm.

Youth are affected not only by their own struggle with moral values, but also with the struggles of other youth. A peer's cheating to win an academic award teaches youth something about the cost of honesty. A world full of troubles, and Christians sharply disagreeing with one another about the right solutions, teaches youth that the right answer is often hard to see.

Understanding moral behavior is difficult for youth. Comprehending how youth differentiate right and wrong is a difficult task for leaders of youth. This chapter explores three major areas of interest in an attempt to understand youth as moral beings: (1) some ideas about moral development; (2) an examination of the personal and social moral concerns of today's youth; and (3) two significant moral issues that affect American youth: sexuality and substance abuse.

Moral Development

How do youth acquire a system of morality? Does it grow in them, or do they learn it? If they know the right thing to do, does that mean they are likely to do it? The last twenty-five years have brought a great deal of research in these areas—especially by developmental psychologists and educators. Like most research, their results have not led to a uniform conclusion, but much of the understanding about moral development can be divided into some general categories. I want you to consider two.[2]

Theoretical Approaches

We will consider two of these basic approaches to understanding the development of morality. One is a human development perspective and the second is a human learning approach.

Developmental. This approach views moral development as a natural part of growing up. If a child's developmental process is normal, he or she will acquire morality along the way. Like physical development, moral development emerges on its own, as long as there is a significant degree of nurturing. There are a number of theorists who could be categorized into this group. I have grouped two together, even though they differ dramatically in their perspectives.

Lawrence Kohlberg views moral development as a natural consequence of the child's cognitive development and interaction with the world. He has written: "I shall argue that the goal of moral education is the stimulation of the 'natural development' of the individual child's own moral judgment and capacities, thus allowing him to use his own moral judgment to control his behavior."[3] Other theorists argue that a healthy morality will emerge if children are loved and given freedom to be themselves. One extreme view in this perspective is reflected by Abraham Maslow: "Growth takes place when the next step forward is subjectively more delightful, more joyous, more intrinsically satisfying than the previous gratification . . . the only

way we can ever know what is right for us is that it feels better subjectively than any alternative."[4]

Kohlberg and Maslow would disagree sharply about the content, process, and nature of moral education. They would also differ in what they consider morality to be. Their similarity lies primarily in the idea that an individual's morality emerges as part of the ongoing processes of growing up.

Learning. The other theoretical approach argues that morality is something children and youth learn. It does not occur without being taught. Parents and teachers need to instruct children in the values of honesty, integrity, service to others, loving other people, and so on. The process by which children learn the values of an adult society is called *socialization*. Children come into the world without sensitivities, manners, or values. The socialization process transforms the behavior of these children into more adult-like behavior patterns, including adult-like values and beliefs.

B. F. Skinner, a famous and influential American psychologist, represents an extreme position within this group. He has argued that everything is learned, and that people believe and behave in certain ways because they are rewarded for it.[5] They would neither hold certain values nor behave in particular ways if they did not receive some internal or external reward for their belief or action. A more moderate view is reflected in the work of Walter and Harriet Mischel. In "A Cognitive Social-Learning Approach to Morality and Self-Regulation" in *Moral Development and Behavior* by Thomas Lickona, copyright 1976, they have written that individuals must learn both a system of right and wrong ("the individual's conceptions of what he should do" and ways of behaving which reflect the values in the system ("the moral conduct and self-regulatory behaviors required to achieve moral ideals").

These two broad groupings are not a fair technical categorization of moral development theories. There are other, more appropriate, ways to group current thought. These two groupings, however, illustrate the range of approaches which educators maintain.

Facilitating Moral Development

The strategies used by adults to help youth develop as moral persons will depend on the way they think moral development occurs. For instance, consider an example from each of the two groups of theorists: Lawrence Kohlberg's model and the socialization model.

Kohlberg's Stages of Moral Reasoning. Kohlberg has contended that individuals develop through stages in their moral reasoning as they gain experience and mature in their ability to think. At the first stage, individuals conclude that what is wrong is what they get punished for doing. What is right is what does not lead to punishment. Stage two thinkers resolve moral dilemmas differently. They determine the right by what leads to personal advantage. Wrong is contained in action that leads to personal disadvantage. These ways of moral reasoning certainly are inferior to the biblical command for righteousness. Kohlberg has theorized that all people go through these early stages of moral reasoning; and, as they mature, go on to other stages. There are six stages in Kohlberg's theory, and they are summarized as follows.

Summary of Kohlberg's Stages of Moral Reasoning[6]

Moral Stage	What is right?
STAGE 1	To avoid breaking rules backed by punishment; obedience for its own sake. Avoiding physical damage to persons and property.
STAGE 2	Follow rules when it is to someone's personal advantage. Acting to let others meet one's own interest and needs and letting others do the same. Right is also seen in what is fair, what is an equal exchange.
STAGE 3	Living up to what people close to you expect, or to what is typically expected of persons filling a particular role. "Being good" is important, and means having good motives.
STAGE 4	Fulfilling one's duty to society; obeying the laws; contributing to society, group, or institution.
STAGE 5	Most values and rules are relative to a society, and should be upheld, for the most part. Some values, like justice, are not relative and must be maintained in any society.
STAGE 6	Follow self-chosen ethical principles. Follow particular laws or social agreements as they rest on these principles.

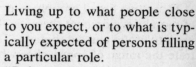

There is considerable substantiation that people do resolve moral dilemmas according to the types that Kohlberg has proposed, although there is also considerable debate about whether stages of moral reasoning are all there is to moral development.

Inasmuch as thinking about moral problems is a developmental sequence, there are several things leaders of youth and parents can do to facilitate that maturing process. One is to provide experiences when the youth is encouraged to think through the moral issues in life. Hypothetical moral problems may be presented, followed by a discussion of the problems. Leaders will resolve the problems with reasoning slightly more advanced than that being used by the group. This will facilitate growth in moral reasoning. Parents who use induction as a primary discipline approach (see chapter 4) tend to have children who use higher stages of moral reasoning. Children whose parents used power assertion or love withdrawal as their primary discipline techniques use lower stages. Moral development is facilitated by helping youth think through the moral implications of their actions and behavior and encouraging them to consider the moral issues involved in the current events in their community and world.

Learning Approaches. This group of approaches contends that moral values and moral behavior are learned. Morality emerges as parents, teachers, or peers instruct youth. The learning needs to be of several kinds. The first involves learning the values that should serve as moral guides. A second kind includes learning how to behave according to those principles, once they are derived. Learning to behave requires learning to resist temptation, to accept the consequences of one's actions, and to feel an appropriate level of guilt for moral transgressions.

Learning theorists have identified a number of strategies that help youth acquire values and behave in ways consistent with them. Modeling is one way youth learn. Adults who have the love and trust of youth serve as models—whether they intend to or not. They are people youth look up to, whose attitudes and behaviors youth will imitate. If models hold fast to gospel values, youth have an opportunity to experience faith as they follow the lead of the adult model. Discussion is another important strategy. Youth need to talk through the moral issues, examine different viewpoints, and be able to defend their own values. The use of reinforcement constitutes a third strategy. Research has established that individuals tend to do the things for which they receive positive reinforcement. There are forms of reinforcement which are quite consistent with the Christian gospel, and gospel behaviors which should be reinforced.

Ways to Help. I have emphasized only a few points from what is known about moral development. Youth leaders can facilitate youth's development of morality. Following are some guidelines to keep in mind as you work with youth.

● Help youth see the moral issues in their lives, church, community, and world. Youth need to be led to be sensitive to the moral concerns because they sometimes overlook them.

● Live your own life with a clear moral stance. Youth learn from discussions, but they also learn as they see moral people. Help youth see other people who have developed a clear sense of moral values and have learned to live by those values.

● Help youth explore the consequences of their actions for others. Encourage youth to accept an appropriate amount of responsibility for their actions.

● Give encouragement and praise. Express appreciation when youth affirm gospel values and grow in their ability to live by them.

Youth leaders can't make youth moral. Parents can't either. Even God does not force his children to be moral. Leaders can create an environment and a style of relationship that encourages youth to explore their values, determine the values most consistent with the Christian gospel, and give youth all the guidance they will accept.

Personal and Social Moral Concerns

Moral values sometimes are categorized into those that deal with personal life (sexual conduct, honesty, integrity, drug abuse, alcohol abuse, etc.) and those that deal with the rights and wrongs in a society (issues of justice, war, human rights, etc). Youth hold attitudes in each category. Some youth have a sense of both personal and social morality while others have one without the other. Tragically, some youth do not have a sense of right and wrong about personal or social issues. This section focuses on the values youth have expressed concerning both personal and social moral concerns. Statistics showing youth's changing attitudes toward these values are included. The average degree of importance expressed by an *interdenominational* sample of 7,000 youth is set at 50. In 1970-71, there were 2,064 youth involved; 1,321 were involved in '74-'75; 2,774 in '77-'78; and 2,338 in '79-'80.

Some Southern Baptist youth have recorded their feelings in response to statements such as: "The kind of moral decisions I make now will affect my future happiness." "I have found a way of life that gives me direction." "What is right or wrong is only one person's opinion." Statistics showing agreement with statements like the first two, and disagreement with the last statement have been combined to reflect the degree of importance youth place on personal moral concerns. The scores for 1974-75, 1977-78, and 1980-81 do not vary significantly, but all show a greater sense of personal moral responsibility than was true at the beginning of the 1970's.

	70-71	74-75	77-78	80-81
MORAL RESPONSIBILITY				
Degree of importance youth give to being their brother's keeper and living under a sense of God's authority.	51.0	56.6	55.0	55.4

If these data reflect an accurate picture of churchgoing Southern Baptist youth, it is fair to conclude that they hold dearly to personal moral responsibility. That would be expected. Southern Baptists are Christians who affirm the Bible's call to personal salvation, personal responsibility, and personal moral responsibility.

Another way of looking at youth's sense of personal morality is to ask them questions about the kind of life they consider most meaningful. This would include items which ask youth how important "adventure, pleasure, physical appearance, personal power" are for them. Other items ask, How important are such things as "meaningful work, love, wisdom, ethical life"? Youth who rated items in the first set (adventure, etc.) as less important than items in the second set (meaningful work, etc.) were scored as having a more biblically informed understanding of a meaningful life.

	70-71	74-75	77-78	80-81
MEANINGFUL LIFE				
Importance accorded a life of service, responsible living toward others, meaningful work, wisdom, honesty, a relationship with God, and giving and receiving love.	50.5	54.1	50.7	51.7

In this illustration, the scores move around more than they did on the measure of "moral responsibility." A typical degree of agreement with biblical values concerning a meaningful life was registered in 1970-71 and 1977-78. More agreement with those values was given by youth in 1974-75 and 1980-81. Probably, there is no accurate way to interpret these variations. The best explanation is that the different scores do not really reflect movement among the youth. They are more like the pounds some people weigh: one week a little more; another week a little less!

Social Morality

Southern Baptist youth also have had an opportunity to express their feelings about some of the social issues the United States has faced. One of these is the attitudes youth maintain toward people of different nationalities, races, or religions.

HUMAN RELATIONS	*70-71*	*74-75*	*77-78*	*80-81*
Attitudes of openness and kindness toward people of different nationalities, races, or religions.	47.6	51.1	47.9	48.1

With the exception of the 1974-75 group, Southern Baptist youth consistently have reflected less tolerance of other races and religions than is typical of church youth in general. The scores mean that Southern Baptist youth have a slightly greater tendency to agree with statements such as "Jews are more likely than Christians to cheat in business." "People in enemy countries should suffer as they have made others suffer." "I believe that excluding Blacks from church activities would be justified in some communities." The data do not say that Southern Baptist youth are prejudiced. Only a small percentage actually agreed wholeheartedly with these items. Southern Baptist youth, however, consistently have reflected a *slightly* greater tendency to concur with the statements than the interdenominational sample of youth did.

The gospel speaks to the issues of loving neighbor and refraining from showing partiality to others. (See 1 John 4:7; Luke 10:29-37; Jas. 2:1-8.) Southern Baptists have been less inclined to address

142

issues of social morality than issues of personal morality. Southern Baptist youth appear to reflect the teaching and practice of the churches where they came to know faith and learned to practice it. The data suggest that Southern Baptist youth have heard the clear call of Scripture to live lives of personal moral integrity. They may have had less opportunity, however, to hear the call to social morality which emerges from the same Word.

Sexual Expression and Substance Abuse

Sooner or later, a discussion of the morality of today's youth turns to the issues of sexual expression and substance abuse. Both deserve special attention. Both, according to the discussion with older church youth which opened this chapter, are major concerns for youth. This section seeks to identify just how prevalent substance abuse is and what kinds of sexual expression American youth engage in. It also will suggest some things leaders can do to help today's youth in this difficult area.

Prevalence of Substance Abuse

"What is substance abuse?" someone asked me when our church was sponsoring a seminar for youth and adults about it. "Do you mean drugs?" he continued. I answered that it meant drug abuse, but also much more. Sniffing glue, misuse of prescription medicines, and use of illegal substances (which are not drugs, but which alter states of consciousness) are all included under the heading of substance abuse. It's more than the abuse of alcohol or drugs.

The *Monitoring the Future* study of American high school seniors which has been referred to earlier in this book has asked youth about their use of drugs and their attitudes about drug use and users. The answers supplied by the class of 1979 provide a good estimate of the prevalence of substance abuse in the early 1980's. Bear in mind that these data are from a *national sample of 16,654 youth, which includes Christian and non-Christian youth*. The following summary comes from that study.[7]

These reports suggest that the most frequently used substance by American youth is alcohol, followed by tobacco. The next most widely used substance was marijuana. Amphetamines, barbiturates, and quaaludes had been taken (at some time in their lives) by about 15 percent of the youth. The following statistics compare the responses of 1979 high school seniors to 1975 seniors.[8] The compari-

Survey of High School Seniors

Smoke a half to one pack of cigarettes daily 15.0%

Smoked no cigarettes in the last thirty days 66.0%

At some time in their lives, they have had a drink of beer, wine, or liquor....................................... 93.0%

Had 40 or more occasions of drinking during a 12-month period 23.3%

Had 20 to 29 occasions of drinking..................... 13.9%

Had 10 to 19 occasions of drinking..................... 15.9%

Drank enough to "feel pretty high" "most" or "nearly all" of the time they drank 27.6%

Never used marijuana 40.0%

Used marijuana 40 times or more 27.0%

Used marijuana 40 times or more during the last 12 months 17.0%

No marijuana use during the past 12 months 50.0%

Never used LSD.. 90.0%

Never used other psychadelic drugs (like mescaline, PCP) . 90.0%

Never used cocaine 85.0%

Had used cocaine ten or more times..................... 2.0%

Never taken amphetamines (uppers)..................... 75.0%

Never taken quaaludes................................. 92.0%

sons are striking. There was a reported decline in the use of tobacco and LSD. There was an increase in the number of youth who reported using marijuana and alcohol. Data are not available for Southern Baptist youth, but it probably is fair to estimate that fewer Southern Baptists are involved in the use of alcohol and marijuana than would be true for the general population of American youth. Church leaders of youth, however, should not be too quick to conclude that church youth abstain from using alcohol and drugs. Some do not.

Comparison of Usage Between 1975 Seniors and 1979 Seniors

	Percentage of Youth	
	1975	*1979*
Cigarette Smoking		
Not at all	63.2	65.6
Half-pack a week	15.6	14.7
Drinking Alcohol		
Never	9.5	7.0
40 or more occasions in last	19.5	23.3
	52.5	39.6
more ... in last	16.4	22.6
	88.4	90.5
... in last	3.6	2.9

...bstance Abuse

When asked youth wh... uld be done to deter the use of drugs, they gave extremely pessimistic responses. They didn't feel that much of anything would co...ce their friends at school not to drink or use drugs. They ...ught that something scary might do it. ... on psychedelic ...s like LSD and PCP is pretty scary, ... le...... experiment with the 1979 sample reported any usage of th... ...out ... effects of alcohol are far more gradual (except for traffic accidents) and, therefore, less scary to youth. The same is true for ...

In one way it seems that youth are learning what their society is teaching... ...al is an acceptable American drug. Marijuana also is becoming... ...ing acceptable. Youth of the 80's probably cannot expect much encouragement from American society as a whole to abstain from these substances. A life of faith, however, may still be an important resource. Some research suggests that persons most active in church are less likely to use alcohol abusively than the population as a whole.

Sexual Expression

There are two issues to consider in a consideration of youth and sexual expression. The first is the incidence and kind of sexual expression youth engage in, and the second is the attitudes which youth express about their sexual experiences.

In a 1973 nationwide study of youth, Robert Sorensen found that 63 percent of youth thirteen to fifteen years old reported that they were virgins. By contrast, only 36 percent of youth sixteen to nineteen years old reported that they were virgins. Forty-four percent of the males and 30 percent of the females reported they had experienced sexual intercourse prior to age sixteen.[9]

Seventy-two percent of males and 57 percent of females reported that they had experienced sexual intercourse by the age of nineteen. John Conger has compared these data with those of studies from earlier generations and concluded that there has been a large increase in the percentage of females who are sexually experienced while the percentage of sexually experienced adolescent males is about the same as it was for their fathers.[10]

A clear majority of American youth leave high school without their virginity. Like the use of alcohol, nonmarital sexual intercourse seems to be expected, if not approved, in American society. American youth may be behaving according to the prevailing attitudes of many American adults.

Involvement in church and the affirmation of personal religious belief influence the kinds of sexual activity in which youth engage. Sorenson's study revealed that 60 percent of virgins thirteen to nineteen years old reported that they attended religious services fairly often while only 36 percent of nonvirgins said that they attended fairly often. Merton Strommen, in his study of church youth, noted that church youth expressed two problems concerning sexuality. The first is that the majority were bothered "because they allow their feelings to overbalance their values in matters of sexual behavior."[11] That's a *good* problem, because it suggests that youth have ideas about what is right and feel guilty when they transgress their value system. The second problem is less positive: about half the population of church youth found it hard "to defend their moral beliefs, to explain why they believe premarital sex is not okay even when it is an expression of love."[12]

Youth Leader Response

Leaders of church youth should feel encouraged that youth who are involved in church and affirm a personal belief in God are less likely to be sexually active than uninvolved or nonprofessing youth. Leaders need to help youth understand the teaching of the Scriptures and help youth think through the religious implications of their sexual values and behavior. Youth can be helped to develop healthy and normally informed attitudes about sexuality. Following are some things leaders can do.

● Have a positive sense of who they are as sexual beings whom God has created.

● Help youth understand that sexual expression is a good gift which God created for people in covenant relationship to communicate their love.

● Help youth understand the biblical teachings about sexual expression. Sexual union establishes a one-flesh union between husband and wife (Gen. 2:24; Matt. 19:4-6); it provides a basis for unique and profound communication between husband and wife (Gen. 4:1); it is the means for procreation (Gen. 1:28); and it was intended to provide mutual pleasure for wife and husband (Prov. 5:18-19).

● Help youth learn to make decisions about how they will express themselves sexually.

● Share *their* beliefs and convictions regarding sexual expressions.

Youth need to know that the way they express themselves sexually is clearly related to their practice of Christian faith. Sexuality is one of the first gifts of adulthood God gives. It provides the opportunity for youth to explore the meanings of faith, love, and relationship in the midst of human desires and impulses. Youth need to learn to use their faith as a guide and companion in their emerging adulthood.

Another important ministry is the care and nurture of those youth who fail to express their sexuality rightly. Such youth need to be encouraged to seek and experience God's forgiveness. Youth deserve the forgiveness of the church as well. Helping youth develop positive sexuality also includes helping those who learn through failure.

Values and Conflicts

The information in this chapter emphasizes the increasing disparity between the traditional values of many American Christians and the values of contemporary American society. There may have been a time when being a good Christian was morally similar to being a good American. Current data suggest that if there was such a time, it is now passing. More and more Baptist youth will need to realize that allegiance to the values of the gospel may make them aliens in their society. The Holy Spirit provides strength to endure the isolation, but youth need to rely on God's help rather than on social pressure.

A second major emphasis in this chapter has been that active church attendance and personal belief do make a difference. Church youth report different degrees of sexual involvement and substance abuse than nonchurch youth report. Leaders of youth are sometimes ready to conclude that nothing is doing any good. It does; it really does. The power of the Holy Spirit really does break through and influence maturing believers. Like all others, youthful believers sometimes fail, and prefer the darkness to the light. They, however, are being touched by the goals of the gospel, and slowly are being transformed by the renewing of their minds (Rom. 12:2).

The faith youth profess and the values they hold are perhaps the most important aspects of development for church leaders of youth. They have been major issues in this book. Youth need to be people of faith and moral integrity. The churches need members whose faith is stable, mature, and growing. The world needs citizens who know what the right is and are ready to live it. That is the overall hope to which leaders of youth are given a chance to contribute. Somehow, the world needs good men and women. The God of grace is anxious to quench the needs of anyone who hungers and thirsts after righteousness.

Personal Learning Activities

Look at the concerns listed on pages 140-42. List the names of three youth you know well. Beside each name, list the stage of moral reasoning you think that person acts upon most of the time.

1.

2.

3.

What strategies have learning theorists suggested for helping youth acquire values and act upon them?

1.

2.

3.

To you, what was most significant from the data of Southern Baptist youth regarding personal morality?

What is the significance of Southern Baptist youth's responses showing less tolerance for persons of other races and religions?

How can adult leaders help youth increase their concern about social morality?

How can/should church youth leaders speak to substance abuse?

What can leaders of youth do to help youth develop healthy and morally informed attitudes about sexuality?

Write a goal or goals you have set for yourself as a youth leader after reading and responding to this book.

Appendix

One way of identifying youth's sensitivities about religion is to ask them how important or valuable they think it is. Questions like these don't lead to much information about a youth and his or her faith, but they do provide an indication of the way youth feel about religion in general.

In a 1981 Gallup poll, "Fifty-seven percent of teens feel that religion is relevant today, while 32 percent maintain that it is outmoded."[1] The percentage of youth who felt that religion is relevant was slightly less than the 65 percent of American adults who, in 1981, felt that religion "can answer all or most of today's problems."[2] In another study of high school seniors, youth reflected a high degree of respect for the contribution religion makes in American life.

In 1979, high school seniors saw the leadership of churches and religious organizations as more honest and less immoral than the leadership of other institutions. Examine the percentages in Table 1, for example.

TABLE 1
Ratings of Honesty and Morality

Youth were asked: To what extent are there problems of dishonesty and immortality in the leadership of . . .?[3]

	Percentage Answering *Considerable or Great*
Large Corporations	37.6
Major Labor Unions	36.6
Nation's Colleges and Universities	20.5
Nation's Public Schools	22.7
Churches and Religious Organizations	20.0
Congress (Senate and House)	37.9
U.S. Supreme Court	24.3

American youth, for the most part, reflect positive feelings about church, and view it as relevant.

An estimate of how efficiently or poorly the churches are doing their work is another indicator of general attitudes toward the churches. The survey asked 3,264 high school graduates in 1979, How good or bad a job do you feel each of the following organizations is doing for the country as a whole? Table 2 shows their responses.

TABLE 2
Ratings of Performance[4]

Organizations	Percentage who said very poorly or poorly	Percentage who said good or very good
Large Corporations	16.6	32.8
Major Labor Unions	20.3	30.8
Nation's Colleges and Universities	3.2	76.8
Nation's Public Schools	20.4	41.7
Churches and Religious Organizations	7.5	57.8
National News Media	11.1	59.8
Congress (Senate and House)	25.8	19.2
U.S. Supreme Court	12.4	32.3

Those seniors said that the best jobs were being done by the colleges and universities, and by the National News Media. Churches were third, and very high on the list. Only 7.5 percent of the youth felt that churches or religious organizations were doing a "poor" or "very poor" job. By comparison, almost 26 percent felt that the Congress was doing a poor job, and 20.4 percent thought the public school system was doing a poor job.

One other way to explore the attitudes of youth is to ask, How much influence *should* these social institutions have? The study of 1979 seniors asked: "Some people think that there ought to be changes in the amount of influence and power that certain organizations have in our society. Do you think the following organizations should have more influence, less influence, or about the same amount of influence as they have now?"[5] Table 3 shows their responses.

151

TABLE 3
The Influence Organizations Should Have

Organizations	Percentage who said less or much less	Percentage who said more or much more
Large Corporations	47.1	10.7
Major Labor Unions	37.9	22.0
Churches and Religious Organizations	12.2	44.3
National News Media	29.1	20.8
Congress (Senate and House)	17.8	31.3
U.S. Supreme Court	10.4	36.2

Implications for Church Youth Leaders

Even though a majority of the youth in the sample were not regular attendees (60% said they attended "once or twice a month," "rarely," or "never"),[6] they still had positive attitudes about the integrity of church leaders, contributions churches make for the good, and the influence they should have in society. This careful study revealed that a positive attitude toward churches existed among older adolescent youth at the beginning of the 1980's. Youth leaders would be *wrong* in assuming that youth do not think church is an important influence and part of their communities.

Outreach efforts should be sensitive to youth's positive attitudes. However positive these attitudes may be, leaders of youth should not interpret them as an eagerness on the part of unchurched youth to become involved. Youth, just like adults, can want more "good" in the world without wanting to give up their own favorite sins.

Southern Baptist Youth

Southern Baptists cooperated in a nationwide, interdenominational study of church youth during 1970-71.[7] Youth answered hundreds of questions which revealed how they thought and felt about many diverse concerns. Since that time, thousands of Southern Baptist youth from hundreds of congregations have continued answering the same questions. Their answers provide a way of comparing Southern Baptist youth to youth across American denominations, and comparing how the attitudes of youth have changed over the years. While data always need to be interpreted cautiously, these data reflect some strong, consistent, and for the most part, encouraging trends in the faith-lives of Southern Baptist youth.

God-Relationship. Several questions in the survey asked youth about the extent of their concern because they are out of touch with God. For example, youth were asked how concerned they were by statements such as: "I lack a deep faith in God." "God does not seem to hear me when I pray." "I do not feel I am close enough to Christ."[8] The chart on page 154 shows how Southern Baptist youth responded during 1970-71, 1974-75, 1977-78, 1980-81. A score of *50* is the average score of the 7,000 youth from all denominations who participated in the 1970-71 study. The scores are from Southern Baptist youth only, and show that the average score of Southern Baptists does not differ very much from the average score of American church youth in general. Also, it is interesting to note that the average degree of concern has changed very little across the years.

Awareness. Another way of exploring youth's feelings about faith is to ask how strongly youth agree with statements such as: "I believe in life after death." "To know Christ is to know God." "I believe there is a personal God." "I believe that God cares for me in a special way." Statement 2 shows the responses of Southern Baptist youth to these questions during 1970-71, 1974-75, 1977-78 and 1980-81. These scores indicate that Southern Baptist youth were inclined to agree more strongly with these items than the interdenominational sample of youth. (Southern Baptist average was 51.4—average of total sample was 50.0.)[9] Youth have demonstrated an increasing degree of agreement with the items across the decade.[10] Southern Baptist youth agreed more strongly than others in 1970-71, and have increased their own degree of agreement over the decade.

The youth who answered these questions feel a close and personal awareness of God's love and involvement in their lives. The terrible predictions that were made in the 1960's about the religious decline of American youth certainly have failed to materialize.

Participation. Another measure of importance of faith is youth's participation in worship and youth programs, and their exercise of personal prayer and Bible reading. As you might have guessed, Southern Baptist youth indicated higher levels of participation in church events than was true of the interdenominational sample of youth. Not only did Southern Baptist youth report more activity than youth of other denominations, but also they reported increasing

153

Concern About Relationship with God

	1970-71	1974-75	1977-78	1980-81
GOD RELATION-SHIP: Degree to which youth are concerned because of a feeling of being out of touch with God and being troubled by it.	50.5	50.7	49.4	49.0
GOD AWARE-NESS: Extent to which youth are aware of God in their lives and believe that he is an ever-present reality.	51.4	54.5	56.2	56.0
BIBLICAL CON-CEPTS: Extent to which youth reject statements of a generalized religion, and in doing so, reflect their perspective of a particular biblical faith.	51.0	58.0	58.0	56.6
RELIGIOUS PAR-TICIPATION: Degree of involvement in the life, faith, and activities of the institutional church.	52.6	56.5	58.3	58.9
NUMBER OF YOUTH	*2064*	*1321*	*2744*	*2338*

amounts of activity across the four sampling periods. The youth who answered the same questions in 1980-81 reported even more participation and involvement in religious life than those surveyed in 1970-71. The data mean, for example, that Southern Baptist high schoolers reported a greater frequency of giving to charity or church from the money they receive, of praying privately, of reading the Bible, and of going to church.

These upward trends over the decade are shared by youth of other denominations as well. The youth appear to be reflecting a general trend in American society. In 1974, for example, 62 percent of adults agreed with a Gallup survey statement that religion can "answer today's problems." In 1981, 65 percent of American adults agreed with the same statement (an increase of three percentage points).[11] While the overall degree of agreement is down from 1957 (when the question was first asked), there is more agreement early in the 1980's than there was early in the 1970's.

Biblical Concepts. Being involved and being aware of God's presence are important parts of faith. They correspond to the concepts of religious behavior and feelings of trust discussed earlier. Still there is another important facet to believing: the content or propositions people regard as true. Several questions in the survey dealt with biblical content. For example, youth responded to statements such as: "The way to be accepted by God is to try sincerely to live a good life." "Salvation depends upon being sincere in whatever you believe." These statements are part of popular beliefs Americans hold, but they are *not true* according to biblical teaching. The more youth are inclined to reject these statements, the higher score they obtain on this scale. Southern Baptist youth were slightly more inclined to reject statements than the ecumenical sample, and grew steadily more inclined to reject them during the decade. Clearly, Southern Baptist youth have a sensitive awareness of the biblical content of their faith, and the sensitivity and precision of their beliefs appear to be increasing.

Conclusions. These data from American high school youth in general, and Southern Baptist high schoolers in particular, give encouragement to people of faith. Youth have a relatively positive regard for the religious establishment in this country. The majority of youth believe that churches have honest leaders and are effective. They also think that churches should have more influence in their communities. Those attitudes tell leaders and Christian youth not to be afraid to carry their faith to unchurched youth. Many have an openness to the claims of faith.

Southern Baptist youth express high degrees of awareness of God's presence, of faithful practice of their Christianity, and of an informed set of beliefs. They need more, no doubt, just like Southern Baptist adults need more. Amid the chatter and cliques that are always a part of youth groups, amid the sins and frustrations of individuals, amid the joys of sometimes silly youth, faith is at work.

---

[1]*Emerging Trends,* Princeton Religious Research Center, 3(3), March, 1981.

[2]*Ibid.*

[3]L. Johnson, J. Bachman and P. O'Malley, *Monitoring the Future: Questionnaire Responses from the Nation's High School Seniors* (Ann Arbor, MI: The University of Michigan, 1980), pp. 106-7.

[4]*Ibid.,* pp. 125-27.

[5]*Ibid.,* pp. 155-56.

[6]*Ibid.,* p. 18.

[7]Merton Strommen, *Five Cries of Youth* (New York: Harper and Row, 1974), p. 117.

[8]Williams, Benson, and Strommen, *Becoming the Gift* (survey) (Nashville: The Sunday School Board, 1975), pp. 4,6.

[9]*Emerging Trends,* March 1981.

[10]Dean Hoge and Negory Petrillo, "Determinants of Church Participation Among High School Youth," *Journal for the Scientific Study of Religion,* 17(4), Dec. 1978, pp. 359-80.

[11]*Emerging Trends,* March 1981.

Notes

CHAPTER 1

[1]From the *Revised Standard Version of the Bible,* copyrighted 1946, 1952, © 1971, 1973 by the Division of Christian Education of the National Council of the Churches of Christ in the U.S.A., and used by permission. Subsequent quotations are marked RSV.

CHAPTER 2

[1]David Bakan, "Adolescence in America: From Idea to Social Fact," in Thomas Cottle (ed.), *Readings in Adolescent Psychology: Contemporary Perspectives* (New York: Harper and Row, 1977), p. 4.

[2]G. Stanley Hall, *Adolescence: Its Psychology and Its Relations to Physiology, Anthropology, Sociology, Sex, Crime, Religion, and Education* (New York: Appleton and Company, 1904), p. xvi.

[3]Quoted by Dorothy Rogers, in *Adolescence* (Monterey, CA: Brooks/Cole, 1978), p. 2.

[4]*Time Magazine,* June 29, 1981.

[5]B. G. Lambert, B. Rothschild, R. Atland, and L. Green, *Adolescence: Transition from Childhood to Maturity.* Second Edition. (Monterey, CA: Brooks/Cole, 1978), p. 54.

[6]*U.S. News and World Report,* April 16, 1979, p. 27.

[7]*Advertising Age,* April 6, 1981, pp. S-1, S-23.

[8]B. Hill and N. Burke, "Some Disadvantaged Youth Look at Their Schools," *Journal of Negro Education,* Spring 1968.

[9]L. Johnston, J. Backman, and P. O'Malley, *Monitoring the Future* (Ann Arbor, MI: The University of Michigan, 1980).

[10]This is an ongoing investigation, conducted annually. Data from these investigations are referenced extensively and pulled from several pages in the various volumes of *Monitoring the Future,* University of Michigan.

[11]*Monitor Memo* (Nashville: The Sunday School Board, SBC), July 10, 1981.

CHAPTER 3

[1]B. G. Lambert, B. Rothschild, R. Atland, and L. Green, *Adolescence: Transition from Childhood to Maturity,* Second Edition, (Monterey, CA: Brooks/Cole, 1978), p. 114.

[2]John Conger, *Adolescence: Generation Under Pressure.* (New York: Harper and Row, 1979), p. 19.

[3]Lambert, *Adolescence: Transition from Childhood,* pp. 107-9.

[4]*Ibid.,* pp. 118-19.

[5]*Ibid.,* p. 111.

[6]J. Phillips, *Piaget's Theory: A Primer.* (San Francisco: W. H. Freeman Publishers, 1981).

[7]J. Adelson, "The Development of Ideology in Adolescence" quoted by D. Rogers, *Adolescence: A Psychological Perspective* (Monterey, CA: Brooks/Cole, 1978) p. 53.

[8]D. Elkind, "Cognitive Structure and the Adolescent Experience" *Adolescence,* 1967, 2(8), pp. 427-34.

[9]Erik Erikson. *Identity, Youth, and Crisis* (New York, W. W. Norton and Company, Inc., 1968), p. 87.

[10]*Ibid.,* pp. 128-35.

[11]*Ibid.,* p. 129.

[12]*Ibid.,* p. 87.

[13]*Ibid.,* p. 157.

[14]*Ibid.,* p. 157.

[15]P. Blos, "The Second Individuating Process of Adolescence." *The Psychoanalytic Study of the Child,* 1967, (22), pp. 167-86.

[16]Lambert, *Adolescence: Transition,* pp. 161-62.

[17]*Ibid.,* p. 164.

CHAPTER 4

[1]John Conger, *Adolescence: Generation Under Pressure* (New York: Harper and Row, 1979), p. 47.

[2]Robert Havighurst, *Developmental Tasks and Education* (New York: David McKay, 1972), p. 49.

[3]B. Lambert, B. Rothschild, R. Altland, and L. Green, *Adolescence: Transition from Childhood to Maturity* (Monterey, CA: Brooks/Cole, 1978), pp. 42-46.

[4]Conger, *Adolescence: Generation Under.,* pp. 47-48.

[5]Merton P. Strommen, *Five Cries of Youth* (New York: Harper and Row Publishers, 1974), p. 42.

[6]Conger, *Adolescence . . . ,* p. 49.

[7]*Ibid.,* pp. 50-51.

[8]Strommen, *Five Cries of Youth,* p. 45.

[9]Herbert Saltzstein. "Social Influences and Moral Development: A Perspective on

the Role of Parents and Peers" in T. Lickona, *Moral Development and Behavior* (Holt, Rinehart and Winston, 1976), p. 254.

[10]*Ibid.*, p. 254.

[11]*Ibid.*, p. 254.

[12]M. Hoffman and H. Saltzstein, "Parents, Discipline, and the Child's Moral Development," *Journal of Personality and Social Psychology,* 1967, pp. 45-57.

[13]Page Kelly. *Advanced Bible Study* (Nashville: Sunday School Board, SBC), July-Sept., 1981, p. 115.

CHAPTER 5

[1]Merton Strommen. *Five Cries of Youth* (New York: Harper and Row, 1974) p. 22.

[2]M. Strommen. Unpublished data (Minneapolis, MN: Search Institute), 1970-1980.

[3]L. Johnston, J. Bachman and P. O'Malley. *Monitoring the Future: Questionnaire Responses from the Nation's High School Seniors* (Ann Arbor: University of Michigan, 1980) p. 193.

[4]M. Strommen, *Five Cries of Youth,* p. 22.

[5]Henri Nouwen, *Creative Ministry* (New York: Doubleday and Company, 1971).

[6]Donald McNassor, "The Night World of Preadolescence," in T. Cottle (ed.) *Readings in Adolescent Psychology: Contemporary Perspectives* (New York: Harper and Row, 1977), p. 136.

[7]Strommen, *Five Cries of Youth,* p. 22.

[8]McNassor, *Readings in Adolescent Psychology,* p. 137.

[9]Robert Havighurst, *Developmental Tasks and Education* (New York: David McKay, 1972), p. 55.

[10]*Ibid.*, p. 58.

[11]*Ibid.*, p. 59.

[12]*Ibid.*, p. 72.

[13]Statistics were drawn from the *Monitor Memo* (Nashville: The Sunday School Board), July, 1981.

CHAPTER 6

[1]These studies are summarized in B. Lambert, B. Rothschild, R. Atland and L. Green, *Adolescence: Transition from Childhood to Maturity,* Second Edition (Monterey, CA: Brooks/Cole, 1978), pp. 75-77.

[2]Roger Karsk. *Teenagers in the Next America* (Columbia, MD: New Community Press, 1977), pp. 58-59.

[3]Lambert, *Adolescence: Transition,* pp. 70-72.

[4]*Ibid.*, p. 71.

[5]L. Smith and P. Kleine, "The Adolescent and His Society" *Review of Educational Research,* 31 (1966), p. 427.

[6]D. Rogers, *Adolescence: A Psychological Perspective* Monterey, CA: Brooks/Cole, 1978), p. 143.

[7]This information, and the data in Illustration 1 are taken from L. Johnson, J. Bachman, and P. O'Malley, *Monitoring the Future: Questionnaire Responses from the Nation's High School Seniors* (Ann Arbor, MI: The University of Michigan, 1980), pp. 164-65.

[8]Clay Brittain, "Adolescent Choices and Parent-Peer Cross-Pressures," in J. Cottle, ed., *Readings in Adolescent Psychology: Contemporary Perspectives* (New York: Harper and Row, 1977) pp. 163-70.

[9]E. Douvan and J. Adelson. *The Adolescent Experience* (New York: Wiley and Sons, 1966) p. 200.

[10]*Ibid.*, pp. 200-1.

[11]These data are reported by *Johnson, et. al., Monitoring the Future*, pp. 164-5.

CHAPTER 7

[1]William Hendricks, *A Theology for Children* (Nashville: Broadman Press, 1980), p. 174.

[2]Erik Erikson, *Identity, Youth, and Crisis* (New York: W. W. Norton, 1968), p. 106.

[3]Gordon Allport, *The Individual and His Religion,* (New York: The Macmillan Company, 1950), p. 32.

[4]Gisela Konopka in M. Warren, *Youth Ministry* (New York: Paulist Press, 1977), p. 197.

[5]Ronald Goldman, *Religious Thinking from Childhood to Adolescence* (New York: The Seabury Press, 1964), pp. 240-41.

[6]John Westerhoff, III, *Will Our Children Have Faith?* (New York: The Seabury Press, 1976), p. 63.

[7]Sara Little, *Youth, World, and Church* (Richmond: John Knox Press, 1968), p. 11.

[8]Nicholas Wolterstorff, *Educating for Responsible Action* (Grand Rapids: William P. Eerdmans Publishing Company, 1980), p. 14.

[9]Hendricks, *A Theology for Children,* p. 15.

[10]Strommen, *Five Cries of Youth,* p. 140.

[11]*Ibid.*, p. 118.

CHAPTER 8

[1]Richard I. Evans, *Dialogue with Erik Erikson* (New York: Harper and Row, 1967), p. 30.

[2]Nicholas Wolterstorff in *Educating for Responsible Action* (Grand Rapids, MI: William P. Eerdmans Publishing, 1980), pp. 16-29, identifies three theoretical groupings. Thomas Lickona, in *Moral Development and Behavior* (New York: Holt, Rinehart and Winston, 1976) includes a more precise grouping approach.

[3]Lawrence Kohlberg, "Stages of Moral Development," in *Moral Education* edited by C. M. Beck, B. S. Crittenden, and E. V. Sullivan. (Copyright University of Toronto Press, 1971), page 71.

[4]Abraham Maslow, *Toward a Psychology of Being* (New York: VanNorstrand Reinhold, 1968).

[5]B. F. Skinner, *Beyond Freedom and Dignity* (New York: Alfred A. Knopf, Inc., 1972), pp. 105-6.

[6]Adapted from L. Kohlberg, "Moral Stages and Moralization" in T. Likona, *Moral Development and Behavior* (New York: Holt, Rinehart and Winston, 1976), pp. 34-35. Used by permission.

[7]L. Johnson, J. Bachman and P. O'Malley, *Monitoring the Future: Questionnaire Responses of the Nation's High School Seniors* (Ann Arbor, MI: University of Michigan Press, 1980), pp. 25-27.

[8]L. Johnson, *et. al., Monitoring the Future, 1975.*

[9]Robert Sorenson, *Adolescent Sexuality in Contemporary America: Personal Values and Sexual Behavior Ages 13-19* (New York: Harry N. Abrams, Inc., 1973).

[10]John J. Conger, *Adolescence and Youth: Psychological Development in a Changing World* (New York: Harper and Row, 1977), p. 288.

[11]Merton Strommen, *Five Cries of Youth* (New York: Harper and Row, 1974), p. 142.

[12]*Ibid.*, p. 142.

The Church Study Course
The Church Study Course is a Southern Baptist educational system consisting of short courses for adults and youth combined with a credit and recognition system. More than 500 courses are available in 23 subject areas. Credit is awarded for each course completed. These credits may be applied to one or more of the 100 plus diploma plans in the recognition system.

Complete details about the Church Study Course system, courses available, and diplomas offered may be found in a current copy of the *Church Study Course Catalog* and in the Study Course section of the *Church Materials Catalog*. Study Course materials are available from Baptist Book Stores.

The Church Study Course system is sponsored by the Sunday School Board, Woman's Missionary Union, and Brotherhood Commission of the Southern Baptist Convention.

How to Request Credit for this Course
Adults and youth can earn study course credit through individual or group study.

This book is a text for course 12002 in the subject area Age Division and Special Group Characteristics.

This course is designed for five hours of group study. Credit is awarded for attending class sessions and reading the book. A person who is absent for one or more sessions must complete the Personal Learning Activities for the material missed. A person desiring credit for individual study should read the book and complete the Personal Learning Activities in the conclusion of each chapter.

After the course is completed, the teacher, the study course clerk, or any person designated by the church should complete Form 725 (Church Study Course Enrollment/Credit Request) and send it to the Awards Office, 127 Ninth Avenue North, Nashville, Tennessee 37234. Individuals also may request credit by mailing the form to the Awards Office.

A record of your awards will be maintained by the Awards Office. Twice a year copies will be sent to churches for distribution to members.